AWESOME
BRAIN GAMES
FOR KIDS

AWESOME BRAIN GAMES FOR KIDS

STEAM PUZZLES AND FACTS FOR CURIOUS MINDS

TORI CAMERON

ROCKRIDGE
PRESS

TO MY HUSBAND, MITCH, AND MY CHILDREN, RAYNER AND JAMIE.

Interior Designer & Cover Designer: Emma Hall
Art Producer: Hillary Frileck
Editor: Erin Nelson
Production Editor: Ashley Polikoff
Designed and Illustrated by Creative Giant Inc. Mike Thomas, Chris Dickey, Paul Tutrone, with Craig Rousseau

ISBN: 978-1-64152-751-4

R0

CONTENTS

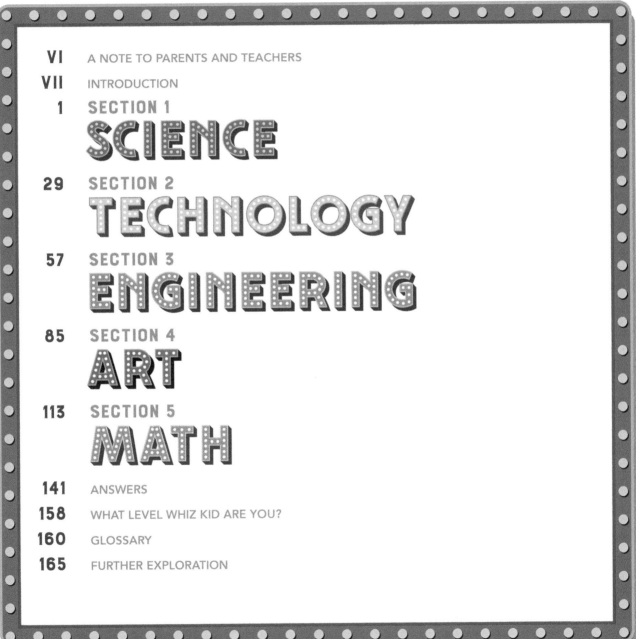

A NOTE TO PARENTS AND TEACHERS

This book is a great way to explore STEAM—which stands for Science, Technology, Engineering, Arts, and Mathematics—with your child or student. In today's world, STEAM provides the building blocks for kids to develop their creative problem-solving skills. The games here aim to bolster a confident, can-do attitude, and prepare kids for the exciting challenges their generation will face.

The structure of this book dedicates one section per subject, but there is no wrong way to explore. Treat each section as a lesson or encourage your eager student to bounce around. The sections include thought-provoking questions to help your child expand their understanding of the subject matter and to think critically about the world around them. The spotlight leaders you'll find here put these skills into action and will hopefully serve as a source of inspiration.

The goal of this book is not to get each question right. It is to encourage kids to have fun as they work through challenging problems and for us to always, always reward curiosity and perseverance above all else. You might even learn a little something alongside your budding Einstein!

INTRODUCTION

When you think about it, STEAM is all around us. It can be found in nature, on your walk or ride to school, and even in video games.

As humans, we think creatively to solve problems, develop new inventions, and bring beautiful things to life. When we learn through STEAM, we get to explore across subject areas, think in ways that are new and exciting, and use all sides of our brains. The best part? Anyone can learn through STEAM!

This book focuses on one subject area per section, but there is no wrong way to explore. Tackle one section at a time or bop around and see what sparks your interest. Inside, you'll find Q&As which answer questions that everyday kids like you have. You'll even find stories about extraordinary people who have helped advance STEAM.

While you're having fun with this book, keep in mind that there is another game within to challenge you: Each puzzle has a certain number of points. When you finish all the puzzles, tally your points to see what level Whiz Kid you are! The most important rule is that everyone who tries, wins. Test your knowledge, learn new facts you can share with your family and friends, and most of all, have fun.

FULL STEAM AHEAD!

SECTION 1
SCIENCE

THE BILL NYE CHALLENGE

You have probably heard of Bill Nye because of his television show, *Bill Nye the Science Guy*. But did you know that Bill Nye has also made important **contributions** to science? He created a part for 747 airplanes. He also helped invent the MarsDial, a sundial on the Mars rovers used to travel around planet Mars, searching for clues of the presence of water. Bill even **patented** a ballet slipper to better support dancers' feet and toes when dancing *en pointe*!

This section is named after Bill Nye because of the clever ways he gets us to think about science. Here you will test your science skills by exploring games that expand your mind on topics like biology, chemistry, geology, and astronomy. The games and questions will push your limits to problem-solve and think critically. But don't worry, you'll see just how fun it can be to break codes, crack riddles, and so much more! As Bill would say, "Science is the best idea humans have ever had."

WHAT TYPE OF SCIENTIST ARE YOU?

There are lots of different types of scientists. What type of scientist do you want to be?

DIRECTIONS: Learn about scientists by matching each of them to what they study.

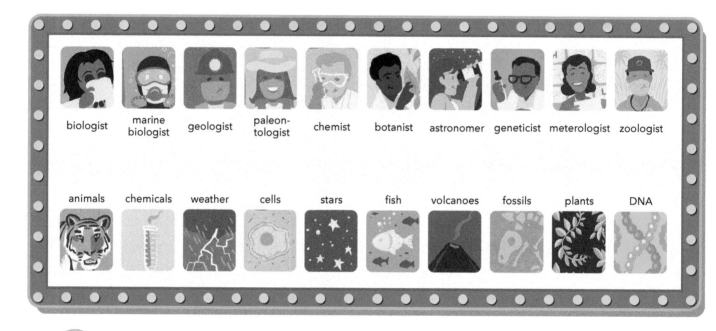

biologist | marine biologist | geologist | paleon-tologist | chemist | botanist | astronomer | geneticist | meterologist | zoologist

animals | chemicals | weather | cells | stars | fish | volcanoes | fossils | plants | DNA

Q You are a scientist who works on a ship. Sometimes you wear scuba gear to get a better look at marine life.

What type of scientist are you?

A You are a marine biologist. Marine biologists study how marine organisms interact in the different **ecosystems** in the ocean. There are many types of organisms living in the ocean, including sea mammals, coral, plankton, fish, and so much more!

PEEKING INSIDE OF THE EARTH

Have you ever wondered what causes an earthquake or what the inside of Earth looks like?

DIRECTIONS: Complete this crossword using the words below to learn about geology.

convergent	core	crust	divergent	earthquake	mantle
mountains	seven	tectonic plates	transform	tsunami	volcano

ACROSS

1. Tectonic plates that move apart
2. The innermost layer of the Earth
3. Tectonic plates that come together
4. A large wave that can happen after an underwater earthquake
5. The layer of the Earth beneath the crust

DOWN

6. Lava erupts out of this type of mountain
7. Tectonic plates that move side by side
8. Large pieces of the Earth's crust
9. The layer of the Earth we live on
10. The number of tectonic plates on the Earth
11. This happens when tectonic plates move and make the ground shake
12. Much taller than a hill and forms when two tectonic plates come together

Q What causes an earthquake?

A An earthquake is caused by movements in **tectonic plates**. Tectonic plates are giant pieces of the Earth's crust that slowly move across the mantle and rub against each other, forming **boundaries**. When the boundaries move, the force between the tectonic plates causes an earthquake. The different types of tectonic plate boundaries are **transform**, **convergent**, and **divergent**.

LOOK OUT, A HURRICANE!

There is a big hurricane coming to the town nearby. The mayor is worried the beach is going to **erode** and the houses will flood. What can you do to help?

DIRECTIONS: You have four materials to choose from, but you can only use two. Which two materials will help you build a wall against the waves? Draw your two choices on the picture of the town to show how you would use the materials.

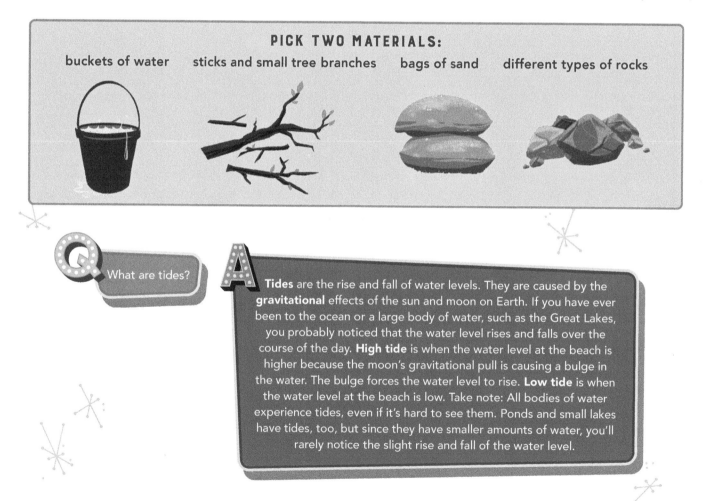

PICK TWO MATERIALS:

buckets of water   sticks and small tree branches   bags of sand   different types of rocks

Q What are tides?

A **Tides** are the rise and fall of water levels. They are caused by the **gravitational** effects of the sun and moon on Earth. If you have ever been to the ocean or a large body of water, such as the Great Lakes, you probably noticed that the water level rises and falls over the course of the day. **High tide** is when the water level at the beach is higher because the moon's gravitational pull is causing a bulge in the water. The bulge forces the water level to rise. **Low tide** is when the water level at the beach is low. Take note: All bodies of water experience tides, even if it's hard to see them. Ponds and small lakes have tides, too, but since they have smaller amounts of water, you'll rarely notice the slight rise and fall of the water level.

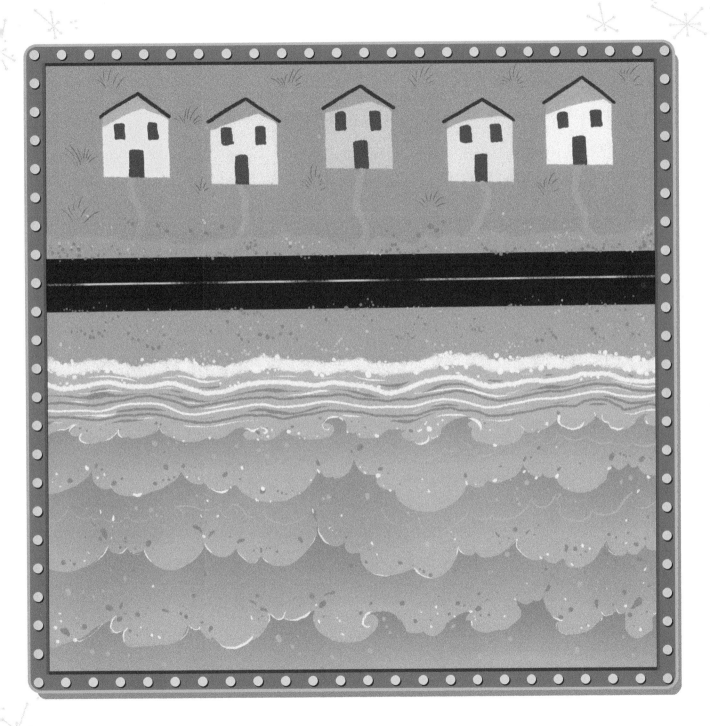

LAVA LOGIC

A volcano is about to **erupt**! However, the magma is having a difficult time traveling through the volcano.

DIRECTIONS: Help the magma make its way from the **upper mantle** through the **crust** to the **surface** of the volcano by completing the maze.

Q Why is Hawaii said to be on a "conveyor belt"?

A Hawaii is located on the Pacific tectonic plate. Also known as the Pacific Plate, it is slowly moving toward the North American Plate at the speed that our fingernails grow! The Hawaiian Islands are made up of **volcanic rock** because they are created by erupting underwater volcanoes. In a very slow manner, new islands are created underwater and eventually come to the ocean's surface. How does all this connect like a conveyor belt? A conveyor belt is a band typically made out of fabric or rubber that moves objects in one direction. You have probably seen a conveyor belt when buying groceries at the supermarket. Because of the creation of new islands and Hawaii's slow movement, it seems like Hawaii is on a conveyor belt.

SCIENTIST SPOTLIGHT

ZELMA MAINE-JACKSON is a geologist who specializes in cleaning up nuclear waste in Washington State's groundwater. Zelma loves to drill cores from Earth's crust so she can learn about the land by looking at its layers. As part of her job, she studies uranium deposits and groundwater.

Zelma is a leader, as she **advocates** for communities that have been negatively affected by hazardous waste and helps to save sea turtles in her home state of South Carolina.

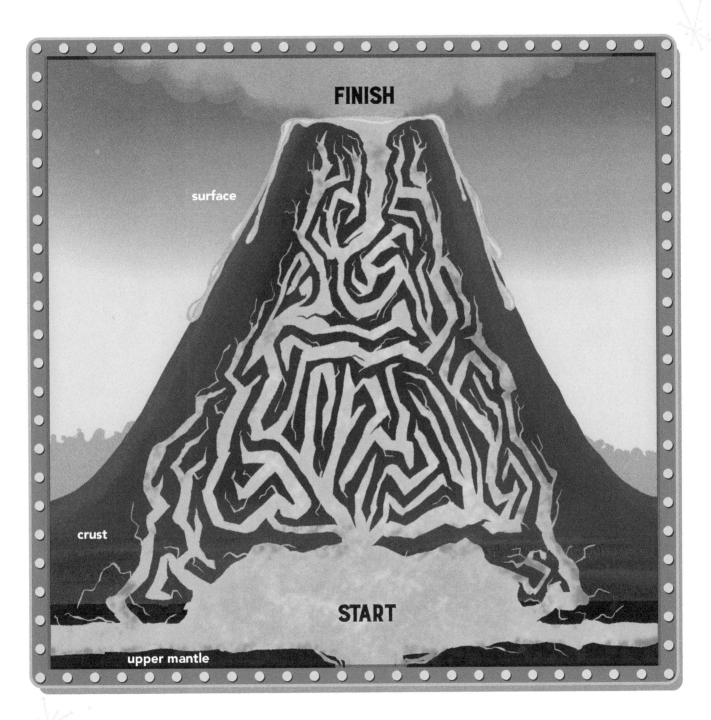

FINISH

surface

crust

START

upper mantle

WHERE ARE THE  MAMMALS?

Mammals are animals that have spines (backbones), breathe air, grow hair, and are warm-blooded.

DIRECTIONS: Look at the picture and find all the mammals. When you find one, circle it.

Q

What is the difference between a biome and an ecosystem?

A The terms biome and ecosystem are sometimes used together to describe areas on Earth. However, the two words have different meanings. A **biome** is used to describe a geographic area based on its climate, temperature, soil, and the types of animals and plants in it. A few examples of biomes are rain forests, tundra, and **deciduous** forests. An **ecosystem** refers to the interaction of the plants and animals in an area. While a biome can be very large and cover lots of landmass, an ecosystem usually refers to a smaller area. A few examples of ecosystems are swamps, coral reefs, mountains, and woodland areas. You can have several different types of ecosystems in one biome.

WORD  SAFARI

Can you uncover the biodiversity terms hidden in the word safari?

DIRECTIONS: Solve the word mystery by matching each letter of the alphabet with a number. Each number will always be paired with the same letter. Use the pictures as clues. Note: Words can be singular or plural.

Use the word provided to help you solve the rest of the riddle!

A	B	C	D	E	F	G	H	I	J	K	L	M	N	O	P	Q	R	S	T	U	V	W	X	Y	Z

STEVEN CHU is a Nobel Prize–winning physicist who created a way to cool and trap **atoms** using light. By doing this, scientists can manipulate atoms—the smallest unit of matter! The discovery led to creating atomic clocks and measuring gravity.

Steven is also an advocate for designing houses and other buildings with white roofs so that light can be reflected into space, therefore helping to lessen global warming. Steven served on President Obama's cabinet as secretary of energy from 2009 to 2013.

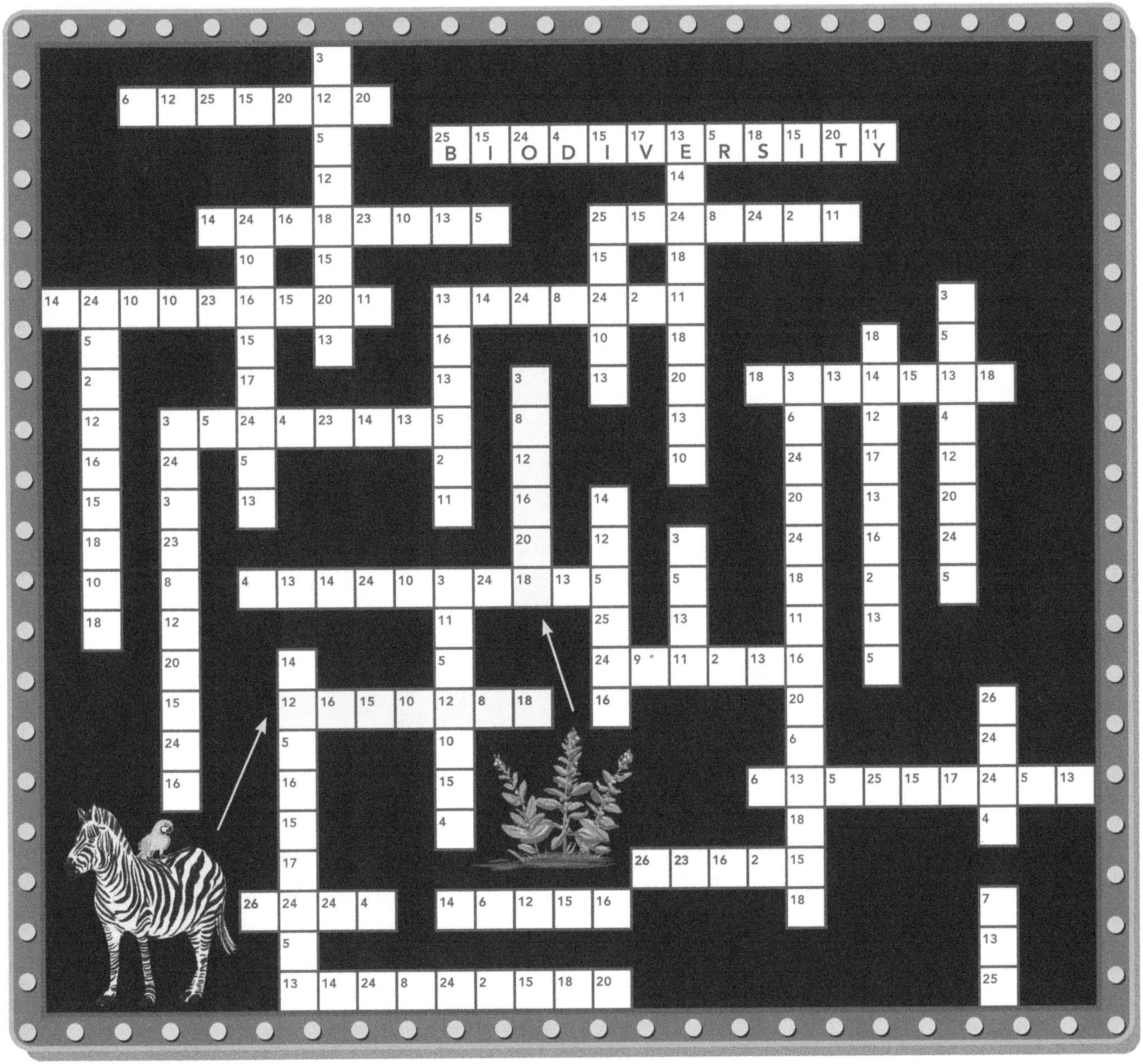
BIODIVERSITY

A TOUGH  TO SWALLOW

Where does each part of the digestive track go?

DIRECTIONS: Use the pictures in the bank to help you draw each part of the digestive system where it belongs.

Q Why do babies have more bones than adults?

A Babies are typically born with about 300 bones, while adults have 206. Where do those extra bones go? The bones don't really go anywhere, but they do change. Babies are born with cartilage that is soft and flexible. As they grow up, some of their cartilage **ossifies** (turns to bone) and some of their bones fuse together. This process makes it seem as though the baby's bones are disappearing, but instead they are fusing together to become stronger as she begins to move and control her body.

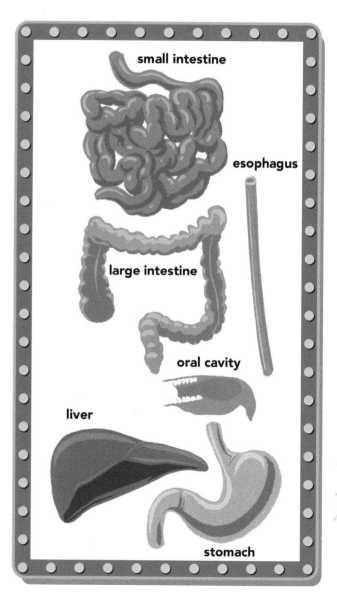

small intestine

esophagus

large intestine

oral cavity

liver

stomach

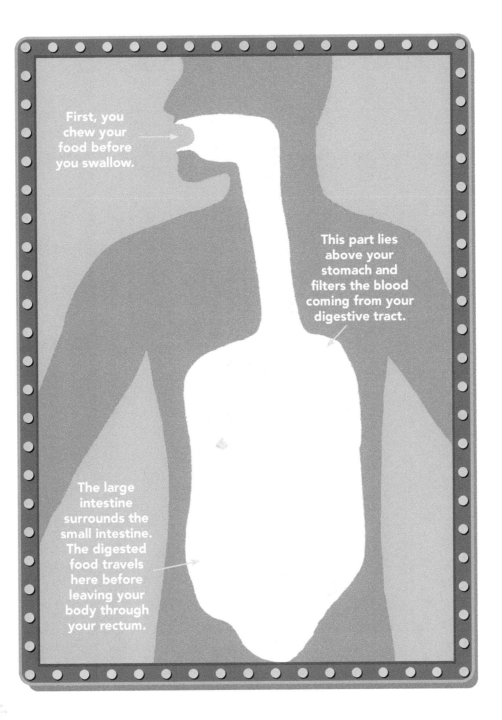

First, you chew your food before you swallow.

This part lies above your stomach and filters the blood coming from your digestive tract.

The large intestine surrounds the small intestine. The digested food travels here before leaving your body through your rectum.

THE TRILLION-CELL SCRAMBLE

Cellular biology is the study of cells and how they function. Why are cells so cool? They make up all living organisms! Human bodies are made up of trillions of cells.

DIRECTIONS: Unscramble the letters below to discover some cell-tastic words. Use the animal and plant cell diagrams for a word bank!

L L E C   N B A E R M E M

_ _ _ _   _ _ _ _ _ _ _ _

C U E U N S L

_ _ _ _ _ _ _

L C L U N O U S E

_ _ _ _ _ _ _ _ _

M P O D N E L I S A C   U L U C I M R E T

_ _ _ _ _ _ _ _ _ _   _ _ _ _ _ _ _ _ _

M O S B O E S I R

_ _ _ _ _ _ _ _

A U O E C L S V

_ _ _ _ _ _ _ _

D N M T O I H C O R I N

_ _ _ _ _ _ _ _ _ _ _ _

L L E C   A L W L

_ _ _ _   _ _ _ _

G G L O I   T P A R A P A U S

_ _ _ _ _   _ _ _ _ _ _ _ _

P S T S A O L R O H C L

_ _ _ _ _ _ _ _ _ _ _

M I A L N A   L E L C

_ _ _ _ _ _   _ _ _ _

N T P L A   L C E L

_ _ _ _ _   _ _ _ _

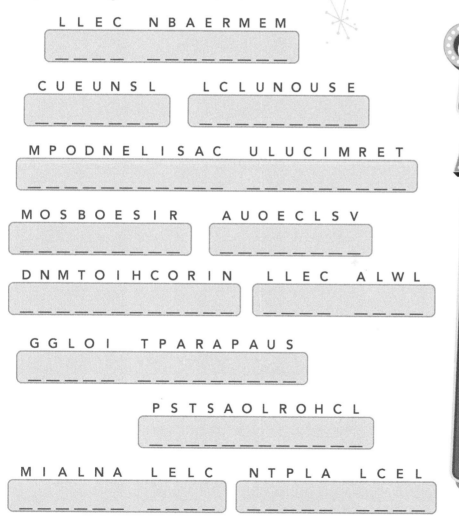

Q How does my heart work?

A The **cardiovascular system**, also called the circulatory system, includes the heart, blood, veins, and arteries. The heart pumps blood through its four chambers. The right **atrium** and left atrium pump blood into the heart, while the right ventricle and the left ventricle pump blood out of the heart. When blood is pumped away from the heart, it travels through arteries. When blood travels to the heart, it travels through veins. Your heart is active when you run, when you sit in class, and even when you sleep!

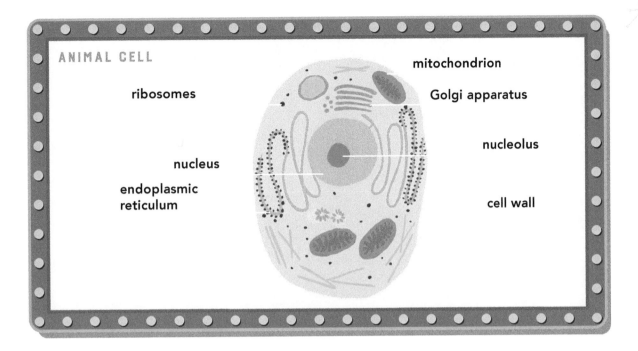

ANIMAL CELL

mitochondrion

ribosomes

Golgi apparatus

nucleolus

nucleus

endoplasmic reticulum

cell wall

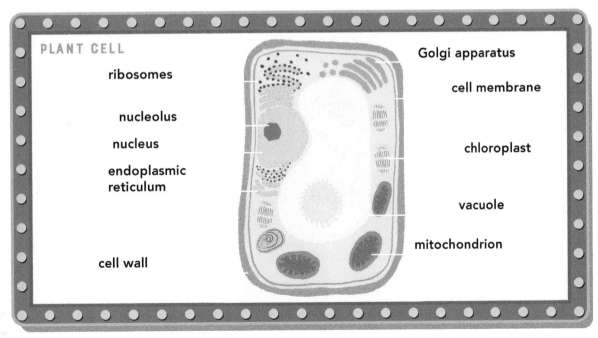

PLANT CELL

ribosomes

Golgi apparatus

cell membrane

nucleolus

nucleus

chloroplast

endoplasmic reticulum

vacuole

cell wall

mitochondrion

BLAST OUT OF THIS WORLD!

Have you ever wondered about space and **astronomy**?
There is so much about space that we still have to learn.

DIRECTIONS: Find the space words in the word search and blast out of this world!

asteroid	crescent	gravity	revolve
astronomy	dwarf	lunar	rotate
atmosphere	Earth	meteor	rover
axis	eclipse	moon	satellite
black hole	full moon	new moon	solar
comet	galaxy	orbit	sun
constellation	gibbous	planet	

Q Why do footprints never leave the moon?

A Footprints always stay on the moon because it has no **atmosphere**. No atmosphere means the moon has no wind or water on its surface. Without wind or water, footprints will never blow or wash away. If you ever get to walk on the moon, you will leave your mark there forever. What a cool space-party trick!

C O N S T E L L A T I O N R E W F G H P
L R R F N M U M O E F R T G A L A X Y U
M F E P L A N E T A E R U O K L R E O T
R E A S R E A T Y R O E T E M M E A U J
F Q T M C T R H I O F I G T O B B F J K
H Y H O U E Q U I V R S U N O E R A O N
E H A S T R N U O E U E R H N A O U P E
Q I T P T A E T A R P H N I W E E E L W
X L M E E R A S T E R O I D S T L A A M
A O S W M A X R T M O Y C O N O J R N O
S A A Q O Y I F N M T X A W H O O T E O
T M T T C N S F L I M O L K L U N H R N
R E E K E E A L V J K E C L I P S E T L
O T L I A R U A E O J A M I E T Y L O P
N R L N R F R E E E L B S U O B B I G E
O E I L T G H O R B I T A B E R F T U L
M R T R R G G I B B L E E T A T O R U T
Y O E E V L O V E R A S E T U M N P O T
G O A E L M N R T S H O L T N B F E D R
R A L O S T H E R E R E H P S O M T A O

LOOKING CLOSELY AT

There are many objects that can be found in space. These two space pictures may look similar, but they have subtle differences.

DIRECTIONS: Look closely and see if you can spot 10 differences. When you see one, circle it!

STEPHEN HAWKING was known for his research in **physics** and **cosmology**— most notably for his theories and research on **black holes** and the Big Bang.

Stephen lived with Amyotrophic Lateral Sclerosis (ALS) and relied on technology for many functions, including communicating and traveling. He was an advocate for people with disabilities and strived to help them gain access to life-changing technologies.

 Why is Earth's nickname the "Blue Planet"?

A Earth's nickname is the Blue Planet because much of its crust (over 70 percent) is covered in water. The water on Earth causes it to look blue from outer space. This is different from other planets in our solar system, which do not have the water we have. Because of all the water, we could even nickname Earth the Water Planet!

SEARCHING FOR SUN

Maya's family bought new **solar panels**. For the first few months, the panels were working well by absorbing energy for their home. However, in the last few weeks, Maya's solar panels have not absorbed as much energy from the sun. Can you find some of the reasons why the solar panels are not working efficiently?

DIRECTIONS: Circle the three problems you see!

How do solar panels work?

A Solar panels use daylight energy to generate electricity. Particles of light called photons, found in daylight, are converted by solar panel cells to electricity. While any daylight can be used, solar panels work most efficiently when direct sunlight beams onto the panels. This means solar panels can work even on cloudy days! However, cloudy days don't generate as much electricity as a sunny day. When installing solar panels, it's best to find a spot in the direct sunlight.

THE TEMPERATURE CHALLENGE

DIRECTIONS: Divya and Alexandria were getting dressed for the day in Canada. After checking the weather, Divya put on her fleece jacket, a hat, and gloves. When she came out of her room, Alexandria was confused and asked Divya why she was dressed in winter clothes. What happened when Divya checked the forecast? Hint: How you read a thermometer might depend on where you live!

Q Why do the leaves change color in the fall?

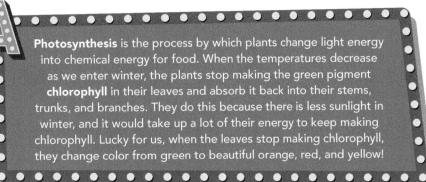

A **Photosynthesis** is the process by which plants change light energy into chemical energy for food. When the temperatures decrease as we enter winter, the plants stop making the green pigment **chlorophyll** in their leaves and absorb it back into their stems, trunks, and branches. They do this because there is less sunlight in winter, and it would take up a lot of their energy to keep making chlorophyll. Lucky for us, when the leaves stop making chlorophyll, they change color from green to beautiful orange, red, and yellow!

SCIENTIST SPOTLIGHT

GINGER ZEE is the chief meteorologist for *Good Morning America*. She is a scientist who studies weather **patterns** and keeps Americans informed on how the weather will affect them.

Not only is Ginger brave enough to report out in the field in any type of weather, including hurricanes and tornados, she is also a supporter of mental health and a children's book author. Ginger is an advocate for women and girls in STEAM and encourages female weather scientists to be called "meteorologists" instead of "weather girls."

LIGHTNING STRIKES!

Did you know that lightning is a big spark of electricity that happens in the atmosphere, usually between clouds, the ground, or the air? In fact, the energy from lightning can create all sorts of lines and shapes in the sky.

DIRECTIONS: Connect the lightning strike from the cloud to the flagpole in the maze below.

CLOSING THE LOOP

Mateo is building a circuit out of wires, a light bulb, and a battery. The wire is not long enough to connect from the battery to the light bulb, so he needs a conductor to help. What material should Mateo choose to close the circuit?

DIRECTIONS: Draw the correct conductor to complete the circuit.

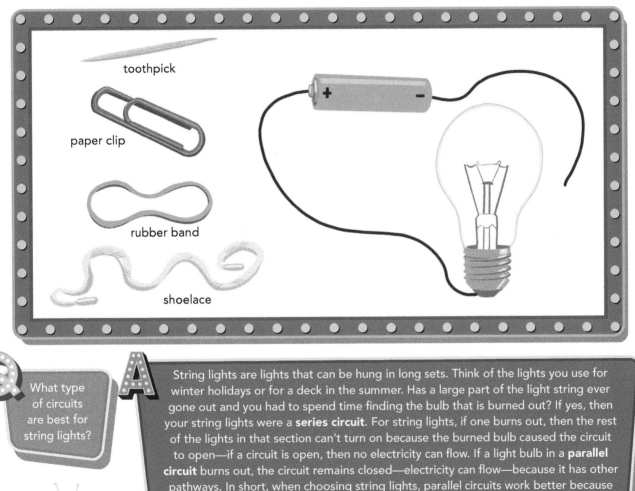

Q What type of circuits are best for string lights?

A String lights are lights that can be hung in long sets. Think of the lights you use for winter holidays or for a deck in the summer. Has a large part of the light string ever gone out and you had to spend time finding the bulb that is burned out? If yes, then your string lights were a **series circuit**. For string lights, if one burns out, then the rest of the lights in that section can't turn on because the burned bulb caused the circuit to open—if a circuit is open, then no electricity can flow. If a light bulb in a **parallel circuit** burns out, the circuit remains closed—electricity can flow—because it has other pathways. In short, when choosing string lights, parallel circuits work better because they won't stop working if one bulb burns out!

A WILD COMBUSTION!

The Chemistry Lab, or "Chem Lab," is where students and professionals of all ages experiment with the way chemicals and compounds interact with each other.

DIRECTIONS: Using the **coordinates** in each puzzle picture, draw a picture on the grid to show where each piece goes. (The drawing doesn't have to be perfect for you to see the reaction!) When you are done drawing, you will see what product results from a chemical reaction when you **combine** active dry yeast, hydrogen peroxide, water, and dish soap!

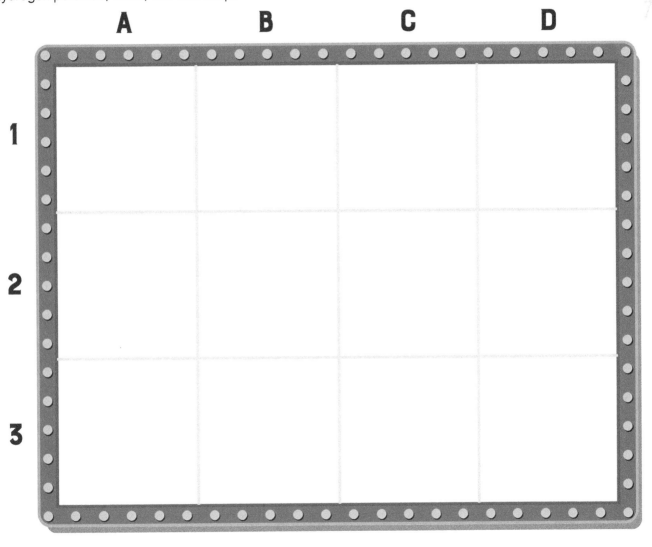

What are the three physical states of water?

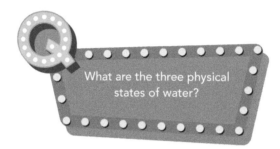

The concept of the three physical states of water, or H_2O, refers to when water is a solid, a liquid, or a gas. One molecule of water is written as H_2O. This means that two hydrogen atoms and one oxygen atom combine to make one molecule of water. When water is solid, the molecules are moving slowly and farther apart. The temperature of the water must be 32 degrees Fahrenheit (0 degrees Celsius) or below for the molecules to slow down enough for the water to freeze. When water is a liquid, it means it is water! When water is heated to 212 degrees Fahrenheit (100 degrees Celsius) or higher, it becomes a gas because molecules are moving quickly and close together. Have you observed water in its three different physical states? Try putting an ice cube in a cup of hot tea!

TECHNOLOGY

THE NATALIA BURINA CHALLENGE

When war broke out in Yugoslavia, Natalia Burina immigrated to the United States. As a young girl in America, she chose to follow her dream to learn more about technology. She went on to create Parable, a popular social media app, and today, Natalia works in Facebook's **Artificial Intelligence** (AI) department, studying data and working with **Machine Learning** (ML).

This section is named after Natalia for her perseverance in technology—a field that long excluded women. Due to her outstanding work, she has been recognized as one of the most powerful female engineers. Natalia continues to advocate for women and minorities in STEAM fields and encourage girls who are interested in science and math to work hard and never give up.

This section requires your determination, just like Natalia. Here you'll test your **programming**, computer, and technological skills. You'll also learn more about how technology has shaped the world in large and small ways. Did you know that shoelaces are considered a piece of technology? As you'll see, tech is full of surprises.

MEET

During the 17th century, Gottfried Wilhelm Leibniz applied the **binary number** system to one of the world's first computers. The binary number system uses two numbers—1s and 0s—to create different kinds of codes. The binary number system then stores the data in your computer—from letters to sounds to colors and more! Each digit is called a **bit**.

DIRECTIONS: You are working in IT with Callie the Computer. Callie is mixing up all her 1s and 0s and needs help sorting out her binary number codes. Fill in the patterns to help Callie the Computer store data.

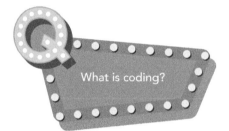

What is coding?

Coding is a set of step-by-step instructions that a computer uses to complete jobs. For example, a washing machine has a set of instructions it follows when you press "regular cycle." The washing machine fills the tub, washes your clothes with soap, rinses, and spins. The code is programmed into the washer so that each time you press the regular cycle button, the machine runs the same way. What's cool about coding is that it allows humans and computers to talk, since both humans and computers can understand code. When you code, you can communicate in many ways. You can code websites, apps, games, music, art, washing machines, microwaves, cars, game systems—you name it!

1. 1 1 0 0 1 1 ☐ ☐

2. 1 ☐ 1 1 0 1 0 ☐ 1 0

3. ☐ ☐ 1 1 0 0 1 1

4. 1 0 0 ☐ 0 0 ☐ 0 0

5. 0 0 0 ☐ 0 0 0 1

6. 1 1 1 ☐ 1 1 1 1

7. 1 0 1 0 ☐ ☐ 1 0

8. 0 0 0 0 ☐ ☐ ☐ ☐

TALKING  COMPUTERS

Computers use **binary numbers** to express letters (among other things). Each letter of the alphabet is expressed using a combination of eight 1s and 0s.

DIRECTIONS: What five-letter word is written in binary code on the next page?

Hint: This word is a greeting.

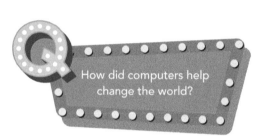

How did computers help change the world?

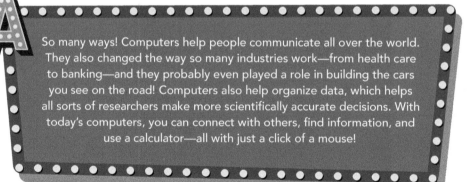

So many ways! Computers help people communicate all over the world. They also changed the way so many industries work—from health care to banking—and they probably even played a role in building the cars you see on the road! Computers also help organize data, which helps all sorts of researchers make more scientifically accurate decisions. With today's computers, you can connect with others, find information, and use a calculator—all with just a click of a mouse!

A	1000001	H	1001000	O	1001111	V	1010110
B	1000010	I	1001001	P	1010000	W	1010111
C	1000011	J	1001010	Q	1010001	X	1011000
D	1000100	K	1001011	R	1010010	Y	1011001
E	1000101	L	1001100	S	1010011	Z	1011010
F	1000110	M	1001101	T	1010100	a	1100001
G	1000111	N	1001110	U	1010101	b	1100010

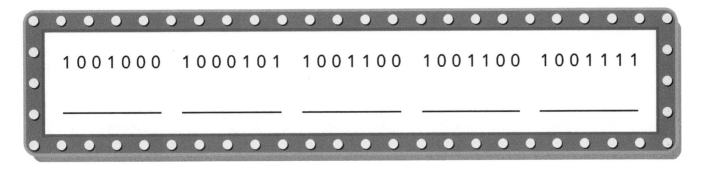

1001000   1000101   1001100   1001100   1001111

_____   _____   _____   _____   _____

COMPUTER SCIENCE

A rebus puzzle uses pictures or symbols to depict meaning. You have to be clever and think outside of the box to make meaning out of what you see!

DIRECTIONS: Challenge yourself to learn computer science vocabulary by solving these rebus puzzles!

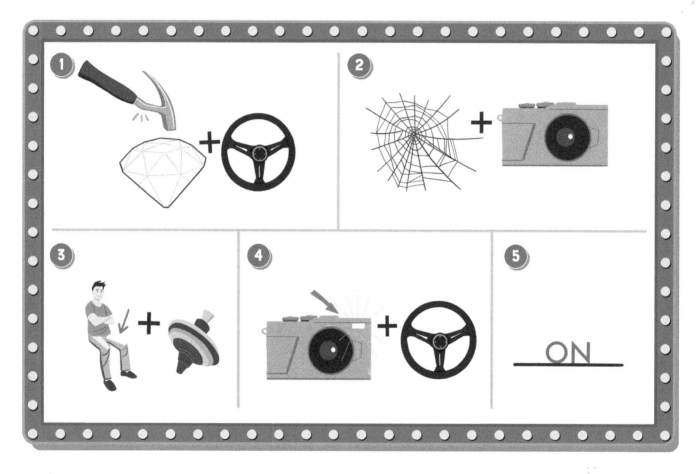

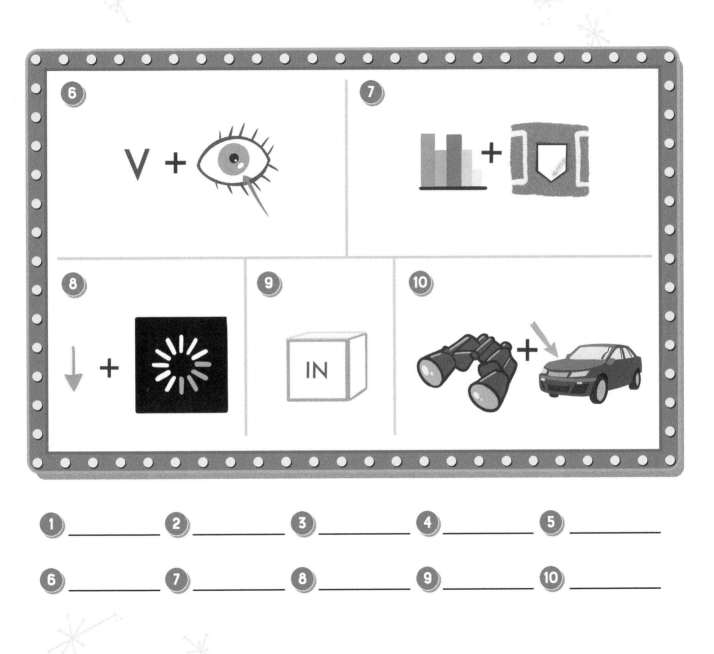

1. _____ 2. _____ 3. _____ 4. _____ 5. _____

6. _____ 7. _____ 8. _____ 9. _____ 10. _____

TECH SCRAMBLE

All of the scrambled words fall under the same technology category.

DIRECTIONS: Unscramble the words. Then take each starred letter and put them all together to determine the secret word.

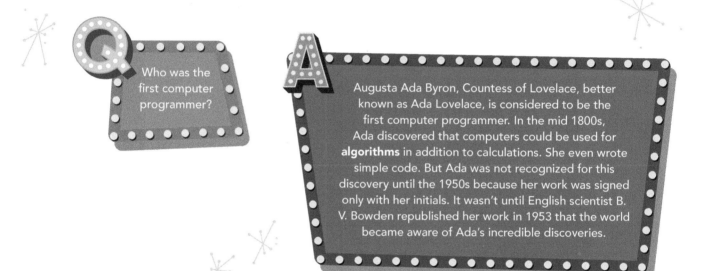

Who was the first computer programmer?

Augusta Ada Byron, Countess of Lovelace, better known as Ada Lovelace, is considered to be the first computer programmer. In the mid 1800s, Ada discovered that computers could be used for **algorithms** in addition to calculations. She even wrote simple code. But Ada was not recognized for this discovery until the 1950s because her work was signed only with her initials. It wasn't until English scientist B. V. Bowden republished her work in 1953 that the world became aware of Ada's incredible discoveries.

TECHNOLOGY TRAILBLAZER

TIM BERNERS-LEE is a computer scientist and engineer who invented what's known today as the Internet. In the 1990s, when Tim was working for CERN (The European Organization for Nuclear Research), Tim made a proposal to build an information-management system. He wanted to create a way that scientists and researchers could share information across universities and research institutes. With the invention of the Internet, Tim Berners-Lee helped bring people together from all over the world in a way that had never been done before.

Have you ever seen a website address start with "www"? That stands for World Wide Web!

1. portumce   _ _ _ _ _ _ _ _

2. tdaa   _ _ _ _

3. tegaosr   _ _ _ _ _ _ _

4. could   _ _ _ _ _

5. sooserpcr   _ _ _ _ _ _ _ _ _

6. daplou   _ _ _ _ _ _

7. creyb   _ _ _ _ _

8. reawlma   _ _ _ _ _ _ _

9. tfreawos   _ _ _ _ _ _ _ _

10. wonodald   _ _ _ _ _ _ _ _

11. eernttni   _ _ _ _ _ _ _ _

12. dowlr ewdi bwe   _ _ _ _ _ _ _ _ _ _ _ _

13. neserc   _ _ _ _ _ _

14. ecod   _ _ _ _

15. itlaidg   _ _ _ _ _ _ _

16. ymemro   _ _ _ _ _ _

17. mstsey   _ _ _ _ _ _

18. podsekt   _ _ _ _ _ _ _

19. altpop   _ _ _ _ _ _

20. knewort   _ _ _ _ _ _ _

_ _ _ _ _ _ _ _ _ _ _ _ _ _ _ _ _

SUPER CODER

When you code a computer, you are giving the computer a set of instructions. Blocks and arrow patterns are a great way to introduce yourself to following a set of instructions, just like a computer.

DIRECTIONS: Use the correct direction to complete the pattern of the code. You can choose from up, right, left, and down.

1. up, down, left, left, up, down, _____, _____

2. down, up, down, up, right, down, up, _____, _____, _____

3. up, down, up, _____, up, down

4. left, right, down, _____, left, right, _____, up

5. _____, left, up, down, right, left, _____, down

What is the difference between coding and programming?

A Coding is the process of writing codes for a computer to read. Programming is the process of creating a program for the computer to run. Coding is the initial step in creating a program. Both coding and programming work together in order to create computer programs and applications. A person who codes is called a coder, and a person who programs is called a programmer. Coders and programmers work together to build information for the computer to read.

KID  CONTROLLER

What is the quickest way for the kid player to reach the game controller?

DIRECTIONS: Draw an arrow in each box of the grid to help the player travel the shortest path. The arrow will indicate which box you will move to next. Note: Your first arrow will be in the box with the kid player.

Q Is a pencil technological?

A Yes! A pencil is considered to be technological because it helps humans solve the problem of needing to write and draw. Can you think of other ways that pencils are useful to humans?

ITCH? NO, IT'S SCRATCH CODING!

Scratch is a type of visual coding language that uses blocks. (It's kind of like LEGO coding!) Scratch is a great way to learn coding, and it helps people think creatively.

DIRECTIONS: Help the student find her way to school by putting the **scratch codes** in **order**. Use the arrows to point you in the right direction. The flag is the starting block, meaning when the flag is clicked the code sequence begins. The red tab is the final block and should be used to end the code. Be sure to notice how the blocks fit together!

Q Can anyone learn to code?

A Learning to code is like learning to read, but instead, you are reading computer language. Learning to code helps you understand how the technology we use works. If your website stops working and you know how to code, most likely you can fix it yourself instead of calling a webmaster. If you think of an idea for an app, you might be able to create the app yourself! If you learn how to code, you open more possibilities for yourself and your future.

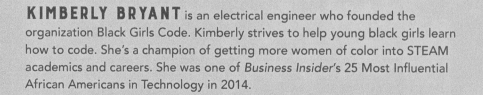

KIMBERLY BRYANT is an electrical engineer who founded the organization Black Girls Code. Kimberly strives to help young black girls learn how to code. She's a champion of getting more women of color into STEAM academics and careers. She was one of *Business Insider*'s 25 Most Influential African Americans in Technology in 2014.

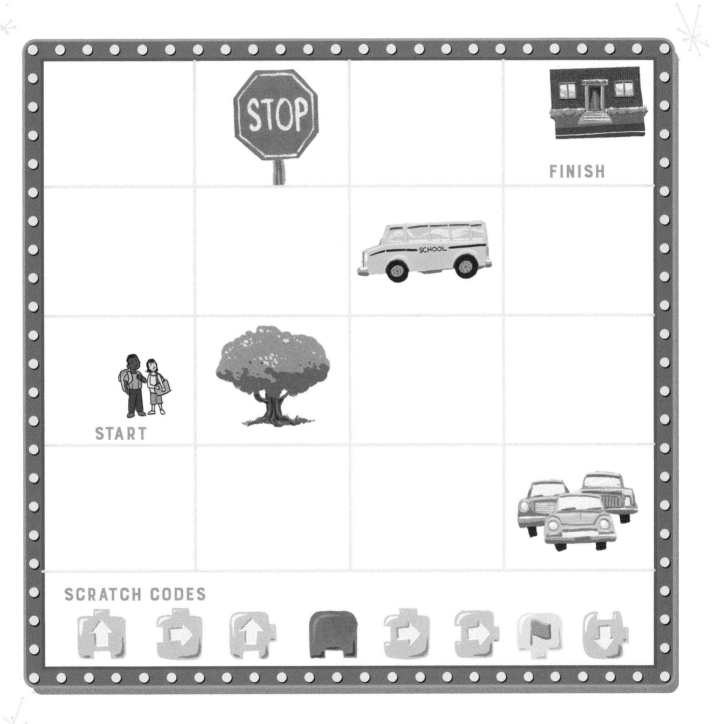

STOP

FINISH

SCHOOL

START

SCRATCH CODES

3-D PRINTING GALORE

Have you ever used a 3-D printer? 3-D printers have lots of different features that allow them to turn a **computer-aided design** (CAD) into a physical, three-dimensional object.

 DIRECTIONS: Using the word bank, complete the crossword to learn more about the concepts that power 3-D printing.

ACROSS

1. A type of manufacturing that creates an object by layering materials
2. Locations that tell the 3-D printer where to print
3. Computer-aided design
4. Materials printed in rows on top of each other to form the object
5. The process of taking a 3-D drawing file and converting it to be ready for printing

DOWN

6. The grid where the 3-D drawing is created using CAD
7. The part of the 3-D printer where the filament comes out
8. Where the printer head moves in order to accurately print the object
9. A wire-type material used for 3-D printing
10. An object in the real world that has length, width, and height

WORD BANK

additive   CAD   coordinates   extruder   filament   layers

positioning   slicing   three-dimensional   work plane

How does a cryptogram work? Each letter of the alphabet is associated with a number. Your job is to figure out the letter that belongs to the number to decode the hidden phrase. Cryptograms are tricky, but the best way to attack them is to try, make mistakes, and try again!

DIRECTIONS: Solve the cryptogram to answer the question below.

Q: What are the two most popular video games of all time?

A: The two best-selling video games to date are *Minecraft* and *Tetris*!

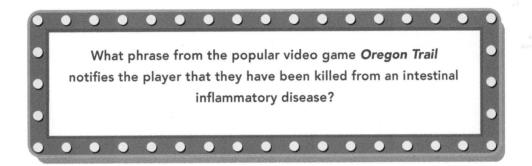

What phrase from the popular video game *Oregon Trail* notifies the player that they have been killed from an intestinal inflammatory disease?

A	B	C	D	E	F	G	H	I	J	K	L	M	N	O	P	Q	R	S	T	U	V	W	X	Y	Z
14			8	10	22		12	18			25	7	9			21	4	3	6	17			5	

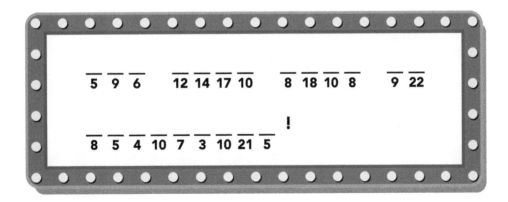

$$\overline{5}\ \overline{9}\ \overline{6}\quad \overline{12}\ \overline{14}\ \overline{17}\ \overline{10}\quad \overline{8}\ \overline{18}\ \overline{10}\ \overline{8}\quad \overline{9}\ \overline{22}$$

$$\overline{8}\ \overline{5}\ \overline{4}\ \overline{10}\ \overline{7}\ \overline{3}\ \overline{10}\ \overline{21}\ \overline{5}\ !$$

WHAT'S YOUR  AVATAR?

Gaming is a fun pastime that can teach us how to think critically and respond to danger (without actually being in danger!). It's also fun!

DIRECTIONS: Discover gaming lingo by solving the word search.

action	console	game	live action	simulation
arcades	controller	gamepads	memory	social
avatar	demo	gamer	multiplayer	system
characters	developer	graphics	open-ended	video
cheat	device	joypad	pixels	
code	educational	joystick	retro gaming	

LUIS VON AHN is from Guatemala and is the cofounder and CEO of Duolingo. Duolingo is an app for learning languages and is used across the world by kids and adults from different backgrounds.

Luis von Ahn is also considered to be one of the founders of crowdsourcing, which is a way that large groups of people can contribute information, share opinions, and raise money.

```
E S T O B C E R T T P E L O S N O C A P
A D S H C H A R A C T E R S S T U B C I
T O O P S E R R C S E H E I R X I P H X
H L P C O A V A T A R J T M C O M P E E
E E T H M T T H I S T A R U L T C R A L
S R E Y A L P U O T O N O L C O N S T S
D M J N K U L P N J U I G A R C A D E S
A C O N T R O L L E R H A T E T U P O P
P Y Y J O Y A R E T M E M I E C I V E D
E I S O C I A L S H R T I O S H N G M E
M J T T U O M L T E X H N N O Y L R O V
A L I V I D E A Y E M L G T O R K A O E
G O C S T O G A M E P K S H H O H P L L
E R K D A P L B T L O M E E K M T H A O
D E M O T P A S R T U N N M O E D I V P
E D U C I G Y M J O Y P A D A M G C O E
D O N T E S R E M E M T H S S O O S I R
A P L O P E N E N D E D C H O I T E H S
R U S H N O I T C A E V I L R E M A G I
M C O L E D U C A T I O N A L O B M K T
```

SPOT THE DIFFERENCE– STEAM LAB

The students at Mitchell Elementary are building low-tech arcade games in the STEAM Lab.

DIRECTIONS: Spot 10 differences between the two pictures.

A In 1972, Magnavox released the Odyssey. The gaming **console** was the first multiplayer video game system and included several programs. The gaming console was originally conceived of by an engineer at Sanders Associates named Ralph Baer, who is known as the "Father of the Video Game." Without him, we would not have the games we know and love today!

FEEL FREE TO FAIL—AND INVENT!

A **makerspace** is a physical place for students to be makers and inventors. In a makerspace, you can create, build, problem-solve, and explore without worrying about failing. Makerspaces can be filled with all kinds of technology, including high-tech objects like coding robots or drones, or low-tech objects such as cardboard or LEGO creations. In a makerspace, you might use your hands to build and create. There is only one rule in a makerspace: There is *no such thing* as a mistake or failure. There is only room for growth and learning!

DIRECTIONS: Unscramble the words to see some of the materials that can be found in a makerspace.

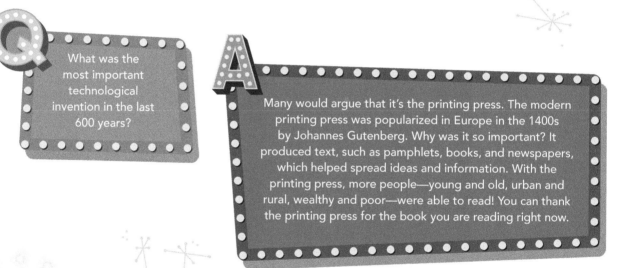

What was the most important technological invention in the last 600 years?

Many would argue that it's the printing press. The modern printing press was popularized in Europe in the 1400s by Johannes Gutenberg. Why was it so important? It produced text, such as pamphlets, books, and newspapers, which helped spread ideas and information. With the printing press, more people—young and old, urban and rural, wealthy and poor—were able to read! You can thank the printing press for the book you are reading right now.

MELINDA GATES is a leader in technology. While working for Microsoft, Melinda helped develop such programs as Encarta and Publisher, and she eventually became general manager of Information Products.

Together with her husband, Microsoft founder Bill Gates, Melinda has made a positive impact around the globe by founding the Bill and Melinda Gates Foundation. The organization is dedicated to changing lives by providing worldwide access to health care and education.

1. ptaecudt   _ _ _ _ _ _ _ _
2. daadbrcor   _ _ _ _ _ _ _ _ _
3. ttliegr   _ _ _ _ _ _ _
4. aeeceiplpnrs   _ _ _ _ _ _ _ _ _ _ _
5. ppiisssolecckt   _ _ _ _ _ _ _ _ _ _ _ _ _
6. sroicsss   _ _ _ _ _ _ _ _
7. lsepcin   _ _ _ _ _ _ _
8. easslitc   _ _ _ _ _ _ _ _
9. sootl   _ _ _ _ _
10. eulrr   _ _ _ _ _
11. gegluun   _ _ _ _ _ _ _
12. ingrts   _ _ _ _ _ _
13. blylcaeescr   _ _ _ _ _ _ _ _ _ _
14. skboo   _ _ _ _ _
15. ckbols   _ _ _ _ _ _
16. cafbri   _ _ _ _ _ _
17. ppoomms   _ _ _ _ _ _ _

FIND THE WORLD'S COOLEST INVENTIONS

You are visiting the World's Coolest Invention Museum. You and your friends are looking at a giant mural of inventions and have challenged each other to find the most inventions.

DIRECTIONS: Look at the picture and circle the inventions you find! There are 23 hidden inventions.

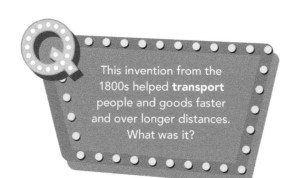

This invention from the 1800s helped **transport** people and goods faster and over longer distances. What was it?

The steam engine train! Also called "the steam locomotive," it connected states and countries through railways. The steam locomotive transported items and people faster and across greater distances than ever before! As the use of steam engine trains became more popular, more railroads and train cars had to be built, creating more jobs. Goods were transported more easily and in larger quantity, which was great for buyers and sellers. People also used trains to explore and settle in new areas.

SEARCHING  HIGH AND LOW

High-tech is technology with advanced characteristics, such as a complex operating system and many materials. Low-tech is technology that is simple, meaning it is easy to use, and it's usually inexpensive.

DIRECTIONS: Sort the pictured objects into high-tech or low-tech. There are 9 high-tech and 9 low-tech objects.

LOW TECH	HIGH TECH
_____	_____
_____	_____
_____	_____
_____	_____
_____	_____
_____	_____
_____	_____
_____	_____
_____	_____

LIGHTNING STRIKES AGAIN!

Benjamin Franklin flew a kite with a metal key attached to it in a lightning storm to prove that lightning was electricity. Imagine if he had his friends join him and the kite strings got tangled!

DIRECTIONS: Help this group of friends by figuring out which lightning strike connects to each kite. Then connect each kite to the person who is flying it. Note: DO NOT try this in real life.

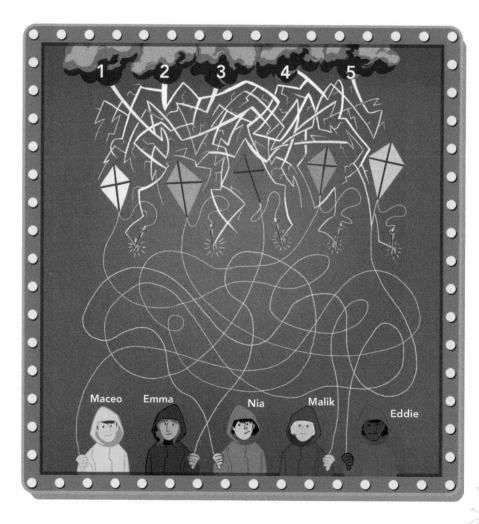

ENGINEERING

THE MAE C. JEMISON CHALLENGE

Mae C. Jemison is a teacher, physician, chemical engineer, and NASA astronaut. She was also the first African American woman to travel to space! After leaving NASA, Mae created her own company, called the Jemison Group, and started her own camp—The Earth We Share—for middle-school children.

This section is named after Mae because she is an incredible STEAM role model, striving to create opportunities for young people to follow their dreams. In a speech Mae gave at the Annual Biomedical Research Conference for Minority Students, she said, "Never be limited by other people's limited imaginations." She has dedicated her life to science, engineering, and making the world a better place.

While there is no one quite like Mae, there are many different types of engineers—those who fly space shuttles, build pipelines, conduct trains, and much more. In this section, you will explore the different fields of engineering while learning how to problem-solve, just like an engineer. You will create Rube Goldberg machines, decode puzzles, and answer engineering questions. You will challenge yourself like engineers do every day.

 **EXPEDITION**

The U.S. Space Shuttle was an orbital space craft run by the National Aeronautics and Space Administration (NASA) from 1981 - 2011. During that time, five U.S. Space Shuttles ran 135 missions into space! In space, crew members launched satellites, set up the Hubble Space Telescope, conducted science experiments, and serviced the International Space Station.

DIRECTIONS: Pretend you are a famous astronaut in history and solve the crossword to discover what each part of the historic space shuttle was used for! Note: For answers that are more than one word, do not include the space in the crossword puzzle.

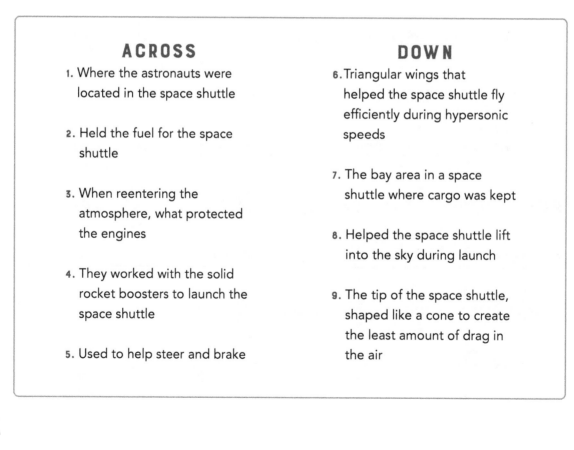

ACROSS

1. Where the astronauts were located in the space shuttle

2. Held the fuel for the space shuttle

3. When reentering the atmosphere, what protected the engines

4. They worked with the solid rocket boosters to launch the space shuttle

5. Used to help steer and brake

DOWN

6. Triangular wings that helped the space shuttle fly efficiently during hypersonic speeds

7. The bay area in a space shuttle where cargo was kept

8. Helped the space shuttle lift into the sky during launch

9. The tip of the space shuttle, shaped like a cone to create the least amount of drag in the air

body flap   delta   external tank   main engines   nose cone
orbiter   payload   rocket booster

# ROVER LOST IN SPACE

Your rover has been traveling from Earth to the moon. However, the astronaut who was going to land the rover called in sick!

DIRECTIONS: Avoid the space obstacles to land the rover on the moon!

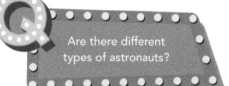

Are there different types of astronauts?

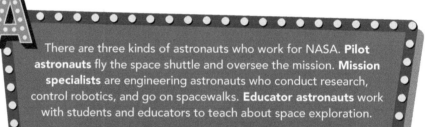

There are three kinds of astronauts who work for NASA. **Pilot astronauts** fly the space shuttle and oversee the mission. **Mission specialists** are engineering astronauts who conduct research, control robotics, and go on spacewalks. **Educator astronauts** work with students and educators to teach about space exploration.

DR. APRILLE ERICSSON-JACKSON, an aerospace engineer, was the first African American woman to receive a **doctorate** degree in engineering from the NASA Goddard Space Flight Center. Aprille has helped NASA design satellites and study the effects of weather patterns such as El Niño.

Through mentoring and speaking, Aprille has worked with outreach programs to inspire interest in and provide support to minorities and women in STEAM fields.

CODE-BREAKER—ENGINEERING EDITION

Part of every engineer's job is to solve problems and break codes.

DIRECTIONS: Solve this code-breaker puzzle by pairing each number with a letter. Use the letter clues to get you started.

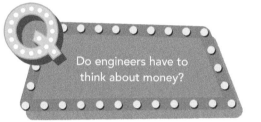

Do engineers have to think about money?

Yes! Engineers are typically given a **budget** when they need to solve a problem, such as finding a way for cars to cross a river, or create something, like a satellite. Resources and materials cost money, and engineers must make sure they are choosing wisely so they do not overspend. Because of this, engineers must learn how to create with restricted budgets and resources, while making sure that what they build is safe.

A **simple machine** is any mechanical device that applies force, like a lever or pulley. Simple machines help us move large objects from one place to another and build things from seesaws to great, big buildings.

DIRECTIONS: Look at the examples of simple machines, then find them in the picture. There are 35 total simple machines. Hint: There might be multiple examples of each machine!

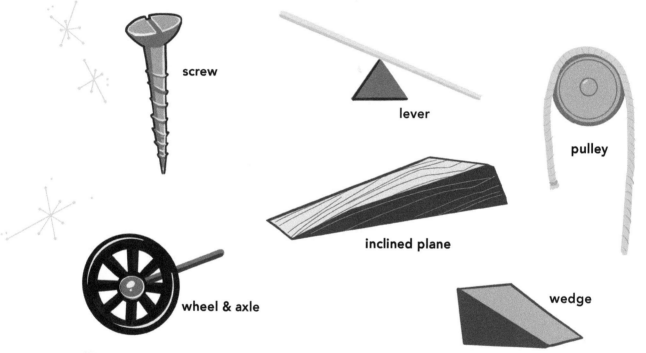

screw

lever

pulley

inclined plane

wheel & axle

wedge

DEBBIE STERLING is the founder and CEO of GoldieBlox. After graduating from Stanford University as one of the few women in her engineering class, Debbie sought to create a toy that would interest girls in engineering and STEAM. She created GoldieBlox, which later went on to win many awards, including 2014 Educational Toy of the Year by the Toy Association. Have you ever played with GoldieBlox?

MASTER OF COMPLEX MACHINES

Rube Goldberg was famous for drawing cartoons of complex machines used to accomplish simple tasks

DIRECTIONS: This Rube Goldberg Machine is designed to help you turn off a light switch. However, there is a piece missing at Step I. Complete the Rube Goldberg Machine by choosing the item from the bank that best fits Step I.

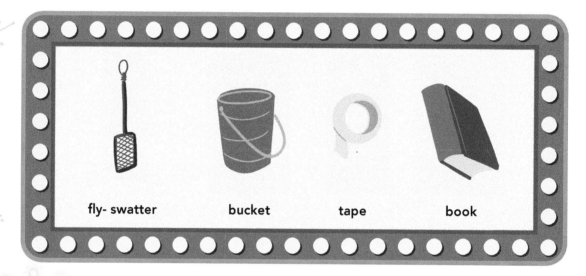

| fly-swatter | bucket | tape | book |

RUBE GOLDBERG was an engineer who started his career at San Francisco's Water and Sewage Department. He soon changed his path to become a cartoonist. Rube Goldberg is famous for his cartoons, which illustrated multistep contraptions built for simple tasks. For example, Rube drew a machine that had 14 steps from start to finish. The machine illustrated a method for wiping your mouth while sipping soup. The steps involve a flying cracker, a parrot, a bucket of water, a rocket, and a clock!

The creations in the cartoons became known as Rube Goldberg Machines. Today, there are competitions, school lessons, and museum exhibits in honor of Rube Goldberg Machines. Have you ever created a Rube Goldberg Machine?

MARBLES ON THE RUN!

Marble runs are a fun way to learn about physics and engineering. When you build a marble run, you design a track for a marble to roll down, like a roller coaster! Can you spot the differences between the two marble runs here?

DIRECTIONS: Take a look at both pictures and circle the 10 differences.

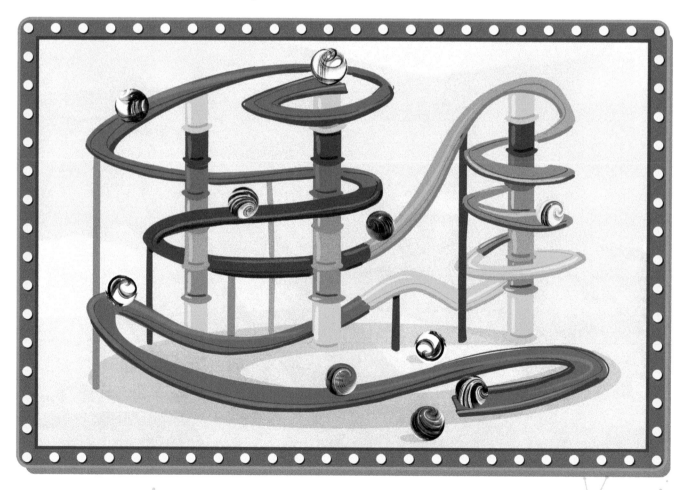

Q What is the fastest roller coaster in the world?

A The fastest roller coaster in the world is called Formula Rossa, and it is in the United Arab Emirates. Its top speed is 150 mph! (Did you know that engineers build roller coasters?)

ROLLER COASTER PRO

Engineers work together to create entertaining amusement park rides so visitors will want to go on the attractions again and again. There are many different types of rides, and each has an exciting name.

DIRECTIONS: Become a roller coaster pro by searching for roller coaster–related names in the puzzle below!

alpine   block
bobsled   brake
chain   coaster
corkscrew   dive
dual   energy
floorless   flying
fourth dimension
hypercoaster
inverted
kinetic   launch
mountain
mine train
pipeline
potential
railway   shuttle
sit-down
slide friction
spinning   steel
steeplechase
suspended
terrain
toboggan
tubular
vertical drop
Virginia reel
wild mouse
wing   wooden

```
M D C D S D U H F B W S S E L R O O L F D E L S B O B L
I E H B T B O Y R W T R E N M L O O T O H L F G T A A A
N U A E E H W A O E D S H U T T L E H U L R H H H U L U
E Y I Y E G K L E Q V N F J G E H G E R I T K U D E E N
T U N E L E T P T U H E T H K N W O D T I S O O E R E C
R R Y J Y Y L L A I T N E T O P I O G H K U D J N T R H
A T Y E N E N A M O U N T A I N L K J D K G E F I H A F
I L U I C R T R Q V F U O I E O O E N I L E P I P N I Y
N L P H H E E E R B B O B S L E D E H M U T G F L M N U
X Z A W Y R D D Y M R R E E T U G G E E I L H G A U I K
Y S B X F A H G N W E B D Y O H T J K N T O T J T J G I
E R Q Y H I O N O I T C I R F E D I L S Q E U F D K R N
Y O U E E L H T G N Q E G S E R M N H I Z W B S E F I E
I L F Q O W A O N G U O P O H E R S G O X A U K T S V T
P B L W T A R O E N M I F C O R U J D N M S L F R G S I
D R Y D O Y R T S A N F O U Q S P T E E U H A T E E H C
E A I H B K I L O N K A L J P T Y G R E N E R W V E J T
J I N H O L R O I H S E R E W T O U D N L U J H N R O T
E E G R G R T N F T R N N O O H T E S U O M D L I W D E
V F O E G J G T E E T D Y S F U G U S D U G E I E O E R
I I F J A F R R J L E T E R F C O R K S C R E W R O T R
D J W D N K O T H D O U Q G H U B D L P A O E K S D H A
K N H R R M L H Y P E R C O A S T E R N H O R L T E N I
O B L O C K A E L O N M P O R D L A C I T R E V O N O N
```

ENGINEERING PARTY

There are many different types of engineers. Each type uses different materials to help them get the job done.

DIRECTIONS: Match the material object to the type of engineer. Draw lines across the table to connect the pairs!

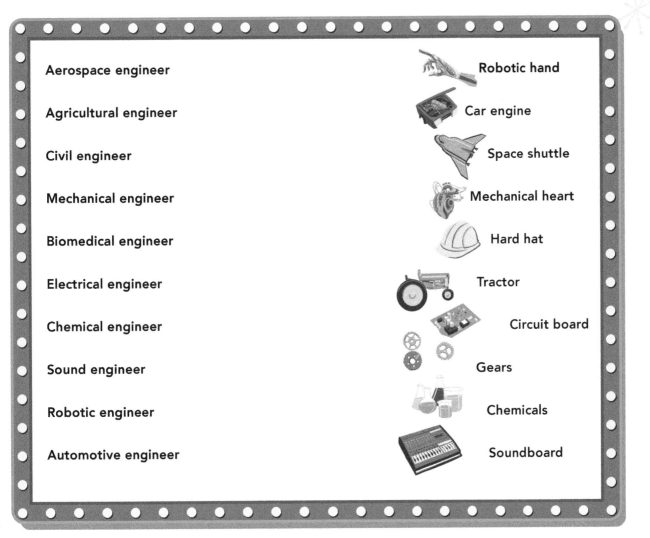

Aerospace engineer	Robotic hand
Agricultural engineer	Car engine
Civil engineer	Space shuttle
Mechanical engineer	Mechanical heart
Biomedical engineer	Hard hat
Electrical engineer	Tractor
Chemical engineer	Circuit board
Sound engineer	Gears
Robotic engineer	Chemicals
Automotive engineer	Soundboard

SAVE THE CITY'S WATER!

GAME 39
LOGIC
15 POINTS

You are a civil engineer who works with the city's water department. The pipes are old, and many need to be replaced.

DIRECTIONS: You must figure out what type of pipe fits in each missing spot in order for the water to be turned on again. Write in the correct pipe piece number in the blanks on the next page.

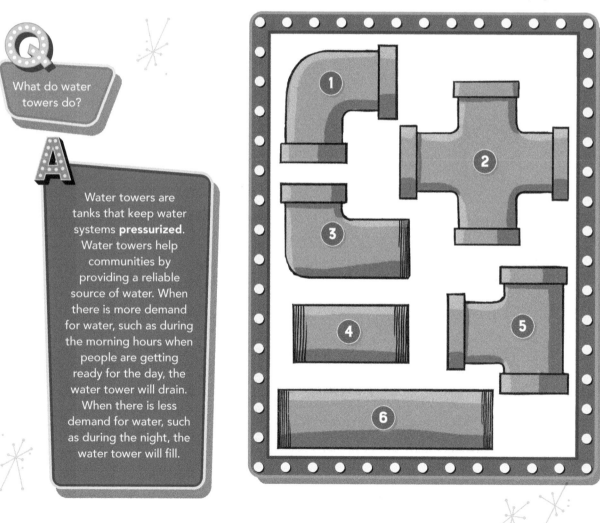

Q What do water towers do?

A Water towers are tanks that keep water systems **pressurized**. Water towers help communities by providing a reliable source of water. When there is more demand for water, such as during the morning hours when people are getting ready for the day, the water tower will drain. When there is less demand for water, such as during the night, the water tower will fill.

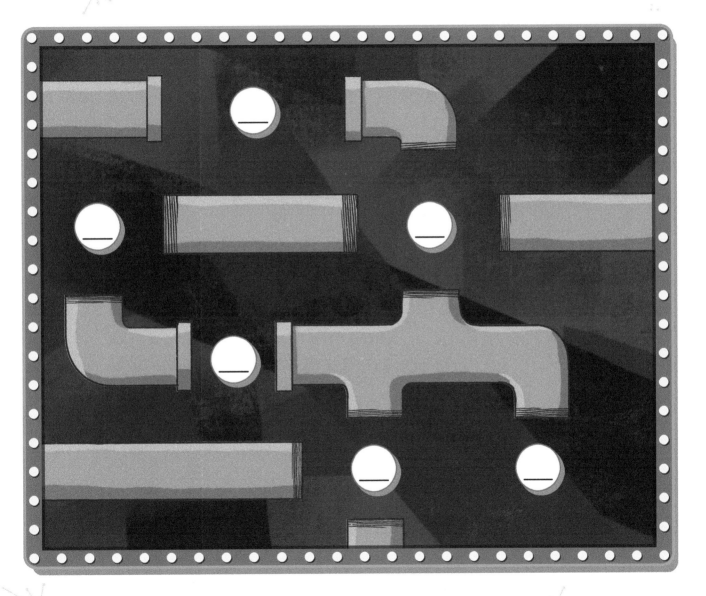

SOLVE THE  CORN MAZE

Agricultural engineering focuses on designing and improving farming equipment and practices. Did you know that building a corn maze takes lots of planning? Farmers typically work out the design and then put it on a grid. Then, they stake flags into the ground to mark the grid and sow the corn, square by square, into the maze. The whole process can take days.

DIRECTIONS: Pretend you are an agricultural engineer. Solve the maze to make sure it's ready for guests to explore!

Q What's one invention that changed farming forever?

A The Archimedes' screw is a machine that raises water from the ground. Water is pumped up by turning the screw. With this device, farmers are able to pump water from bodies of water for their **irrigation** systems. The process is easier and faster than waiting for rain or using rainwater-collection buckets.

START

FINISH

SUPERHEROES OF THE EARTH

DIRECTIONS: You can consider this type of engineer a superhero of today's earth. Unscramble the tiles to find out who they are and what they do. Don't let the colors fool you!

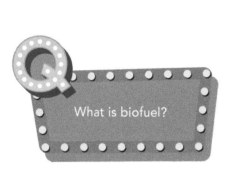

What is biofuel?

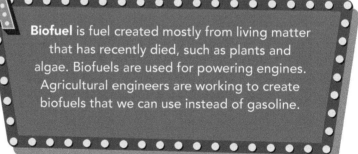

Biofuel is fuel created mostly from living matter that has recently died, such as plants and algae. Biofuels are used for powering engines. Agricultural engineers are working to create biofuels that we can use instead of gasoline.

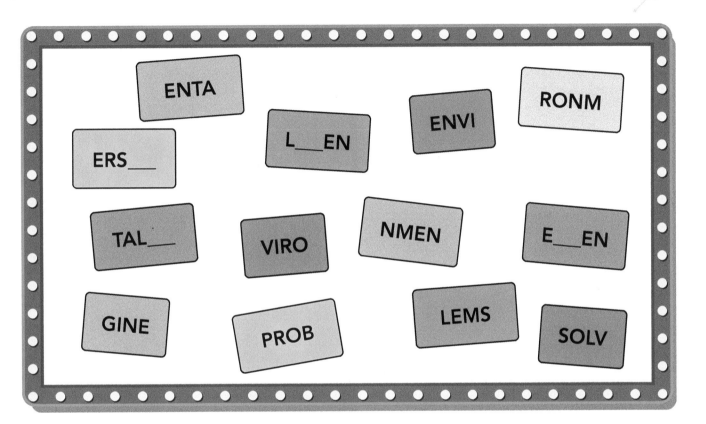

ENTA

ERS___

L__EN

ENVI

RONM

TAL___

VIRO

NMEN

E__EN

GINE

PROB

LEMS

SOLV

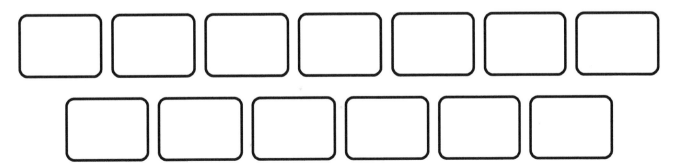

SWISS TRAIN ADVENTURE

Some civil engineers design and maintain train tracks.

DIRECTIONS: Use the box below to help the civil engineers choose the correct tracks to use before the train arrives. Write in the number of the correct piece of track in blank circle.

Q What is a monorail?

A A **monorail** is a type of train that travels using one rail. "Mono" is a prefix that means "one" or "single." Therefore, monorail means one-rail or single-rail. A monorail train can travel on top of the track or below the track. They get their speed from the electric current that flows through the rail. Monorails are typically used to transport people around cities, but you might also spy them in amusement parks, zoos, or airports.

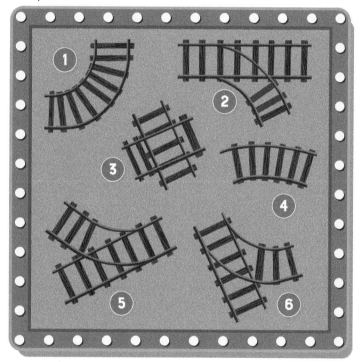

ENGINEERING EXPERT

JOSEPH STRAUSS was an engineer who was famous for building bridges, especially drawbridges. A **drawbridge** is a type of bridge that has a hinge at one end. This allows the bridge to open and close in order to allow things to move under it.

Joseph Strauss built over 400 bridges during his lifetime, but one of his most famous was a red suspension bridge—the Golden Gate Bridge in San Francisco. When the Golden Gate Bridge was completed in 1937, it was the longest in the world!

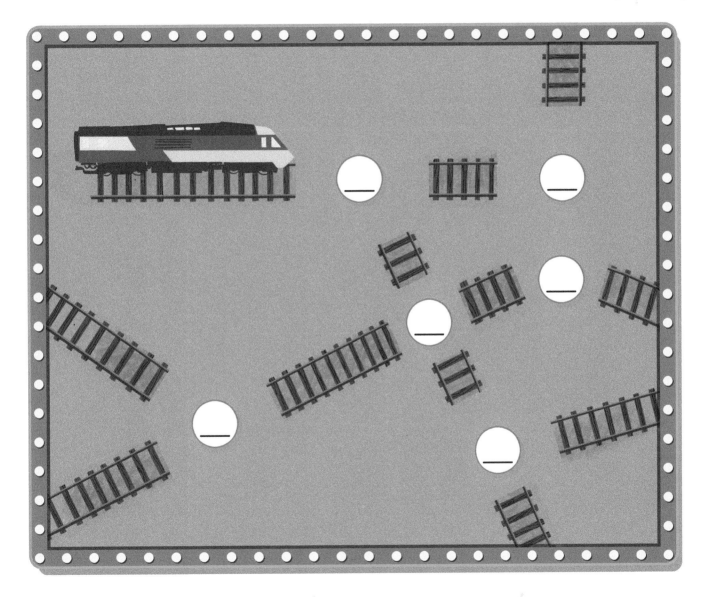

MATTCHING

Engineers have built many bridges around the world. Some bridges are so spectacular, they are visited by people from every country.

DIRECTIONS: Pretend you are on a bridge tour. Read the descriptions of different types of bridges and see if you can match the famous bridges to its type of bridge. Hint: There is more than one famous bridge per bridge type!

ARCH BRIDGE: works by transferring the weight of the bridge and its loads to the space where the arch meets

BRIDGE/TUNNEL: a roadway that includes a combination of tunnels and bridges

CABLE-STAYED BRIDGE: a bridge with cables that run from the deck to at least one tower

CABLE-STAYED SUSPENSION: a bridge that has both cable-stayed features and suspension features

DRAWBRIDGE: opens and closes, often so ships can pass under

SIMPLE-SUSPENSION BRIDGE: an old-school bridge that lies on two parallel load-bearing cables that are anchored at either end

SUSPENSION BRIDGE: the deck is hung below suspension cables on vertical suspenders; it is used to span large distances and can withstand earthquakes

TILT BRIDGE: a movable bridge that rotates at a tilt

TRESTLE BRIDGE: small bridge used for bearing heavy loads; a rigid frame with short spans is used as support

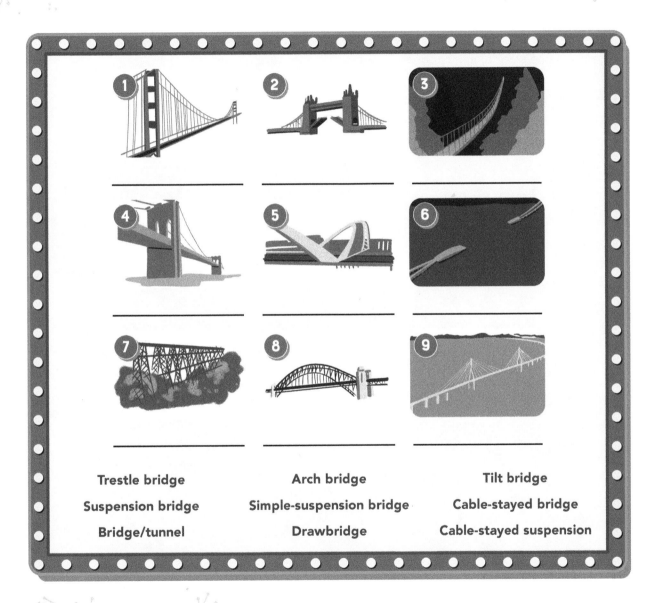

Trestle bridge

Suspension bridge

Bridge/tunnel

Arch bridge

Simple-suspension bridge

Drawbridge

Tilt bridge

Cable-stayed bridge

Cable-stayed suspension

BRIDGES, BRIDGES EVERYWHERE!

There are many different types of bridges, each with its own purpose and mission to help people get from one place to another or do their job.

DIRECTIONS: Observe the location of each picture on the next page. Then determine what type of bridge would best be placed there. (Can you name the bridge types?)

Q Why use a movable bridge?

A When you hear the phrase, you might think of drawbridges during medieval times that were used to cross moats into castles. However, movable bridges are still used today, for many reasons. Movable bridges can be lifted, swung, retracted, titled, and raised. Often, they are used across waterways so that boats or large vessels can travel under. There are many famous movable bridges around the world, including the Tower Bridge in London, England. Have you ever been on or seen a movable bridge?

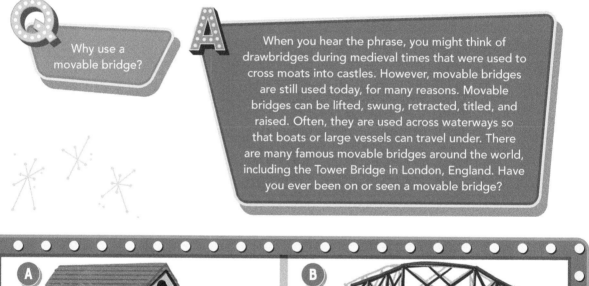

CAN YOU NAME THAT  BRIDGE?

Discover the different bridge types—and their names—by looking closely at the words below.

DIRECTIONS: Search for the words. Remember to look backward and forward!

arch
Baltimore
beam
bowstring
cable-stayed
camelback
cantilever
covered
draw   Fink
floating
Howe
lattice
Parker
Pennsylvania
pontoon
Pratt
slab   steel
suspension
tied arch
truss   Warren
wooden
vertical

```
E R S L A B I N G B O W S T R I N G P Q
R A S B T L T Q U B R E A L M N O M A B
O S I L T M I N P L R O P V W P R A T T
M V C A B L E S T A Y E D S U S B E E O
I E R T T S D P A V N H D E E E H B F I
T R R T O R A A R C I T P L W R G O N B
L T T I L E R T R U S S T O O E W D F P
A I G C N M C A E P F R I I H O S T I A
B C A E U N H L I O A D N J W J K H N R
D A I N A V L Y S N N E P K E O K N K W
E L O O N R I O L T E E O S T C O I O M
R L H C R A I E Y O M N L U A I N D U T
E I A E T N P T O O R E S B S P O N E L
V F Q U L E E T S N T O L N P E R M E N
O T R O O R E U O N A E E L W A R D A P
C A E U E F F H K M M P Q U O R E O B R
E E N K E R U T N A S E A B N N M I N Q
R T R Q U R V B C U O F L O A T I N G U
T A W X O Y T P S L R E V E L I T N A C
P D E W A R R E N N B M C Z E G I J H O
```

SECTION 4
ART

THE HAYAO MIYAZAKI CHALLENGE

Hayao Miyazaki is a Japanese artist known for his incredible talent in the field of animated film. He is well known for his anime movies, many of which have won big awards. His film *Spirited Away* won an Academy Award—the first anime movie to ever win an Oscar! Hayao creates beautiful movies by depicting detailed, colorful images. It's as if nature comes alive, right off the screen!

This section is named after Hayao because his work also brings awareness to environmental justice. His films are loved and admired around the world for their meaningful themes and strong, brave, and curious young characters. His artistic contributions have opened the worlds of anime and Japanese culture to millions of people and have positively influenced the animated film industry.

In this section, you will play games and learn facts about many different styles of art. You will learn from creative artists who express themselves through illustrations, designs, materials, music, and even food! By exploring the many pathways of art, you will open your eyes to the beauty that surrounds you every day. What will you create to change the way that people experience the world?

MUSIC TIME

Did you know that music has patterns that have to do with time? Each note has a value, and that value tells the musician how long to play the note.

DIRECTIONS: Fill in the missing notes using the music notes in the bank.

Is "Ode to Joy" a symphony?

"Ode to Joy" is *part* of Ludwig van Beethoven's Symphony no. 9. It can be heard in the fourth and final part of the symphony, and is one of the best-known pieces of music ever! A little-known fact is that "Ode to Joy" was originally a poem written by Friedrich Schiller, a German poet, philosopher, and historian, in 1785. Beethoven, however, was not inspired by the poem until it was revised in 1808. Symphony no. 9 by Ludwig van Beethoven was first played in 1824. Have you ever listened to "Ode to Joy"?

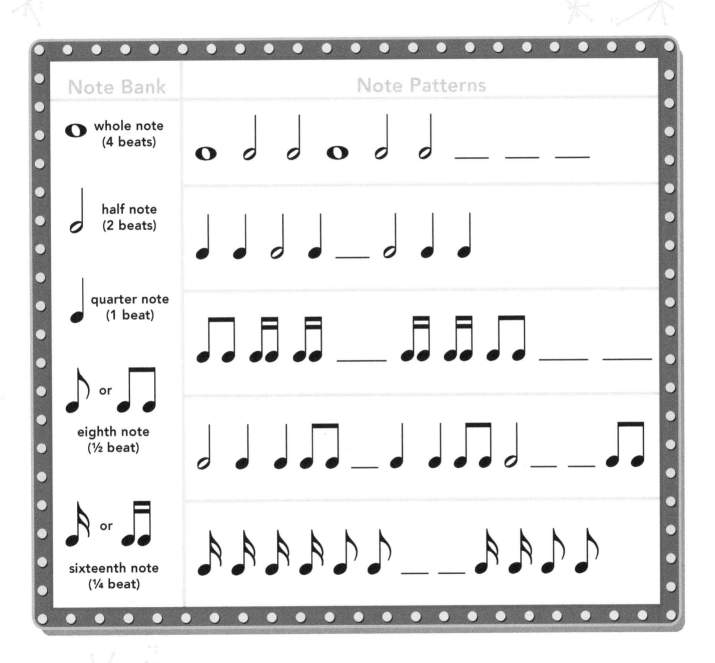

INSTRUMENTS
AROUND THE WORLD

Instruments come from all over the world.

DIRECTIONS: Complete the word search to learn the names of some of them.

banjo	drum	guitar	piano	trumpet
bassoon	flute	harmonica	saxophone	tuba
cello	French horn	harp	timpani	ukulele
clarinet	glockenspiel	mandolin	triangle	violin
cymbal	gong	oboe	trombone	xylophone

Q Are instruments grouped into categories?

A Yes! Instruments are grouped into categories based on the sound they make. **Percussion instruments** make sound when they are hit, shaken, or scratched—the force causes them to vibrate. Some examples are drums, maracas, or the xylophone. **Woodwind instruments** make sound when air is blown through them and the air vibrates inside. Woodwind instruments include the flute, oboe, and clarinet. **Brass instruments** make sound when the musician blows air inside and vibrates their lips. These include the trumpet, trombone, and tuba. **String instruments** make their sound when their strings vibrate from being bowed, plucked, or hit. Think of the guitar, violin, or harp.

LADY GAGA is a musician and performer who has received many accolades, including nine Grammy Awards. She is known for her strong vocals, artistic outfits, lively performances, and her activism.

She started the Born This Way Foundation to support the mental and emotional wellness of young people. The organization helps empower youth to learn life skills by creating safe spaces that inspire bravery.

```
T  I  M  P  A  N  I  E  R  T  S  E  H  I  A  N  T  O  M  T
E  G  J  D  B  D  W  Y  R  O  L  E  A  T  H  R  O  U  E  R
T  U  B  A  E  R  Y  A  I  G  U  I  R  O  E  E  R  E  J  U
R  E  R  G  H  Y  T  O  N  J  C  F  M  B  G  D  T  W  S  T
U  D  F  F  E  I  R  A  E  H  E  A  O  O  H  I  R  V  J  E
M  Q  U  O  U  T  I  S  H  D  L  R  N  E  J  K  H  C  U  N
P  E  T  G  B  R  G  H  O  D  L  I  I  T  S  T  D  L  E  I
E  O  O  M  T  G  J  E  G  H  O  O  C  D  J  R  E  A  R  L
T  S  O  N  F  H  D  G  O  U  M  N  A  V  N  O  G  R  F  O
H  A  N  R  D  E  N  O  H  P  O  L  Y  X  E  M  Y  I  O  D
A  X  A  O  G  D  O  G  E  T  U  Y  R  U  R  B  X  N  O  N
R  O  B  H  P  T  N  C  L  B  S  R  C  M  S  O  Q  E  N  A
M  P  E  H  J  O  T  I  M  P  A  X  C  Y  T  N  U  T  A  M
T  H  U  C  G  M  N  S  F  E  E  S  V  R  M  E  U  T  L  P
H  O  F  N  W  T  F  L  U  T  E  Z  S  O  N  B  M  U  H  R
D  N  H  E  H  K  I  E  U  L  U  D  C  O  R  G  A  L  A  S
E  E  D  R  D  U  K  U  L  E  L  E  X  Y  O  R  T  L  R  C
H  Y  R  F  D  V  I  O  E  O  J  N  A  B  I  N  L  O  P  J
O  O  R  M  O  L  E  I  P  S  N  E  K  C  O  L  G  F  L  T
I  L  N  I  L  O  I  V  E  G  J  G  O  N  A  I  P  E  I  E
```

BEHIND THE CAMERA'S MAGIC

Each part of the camera plays a role in taking the pictures we love to look at again and again.

DIRECTIONS: Unscramble the words to reveal the different parts of a camera. Next, write each letter that is written in a star. Letters will answer the question:

WHAT PROGRAM IS USED TO DIGITALLY EDIT PICTURES?

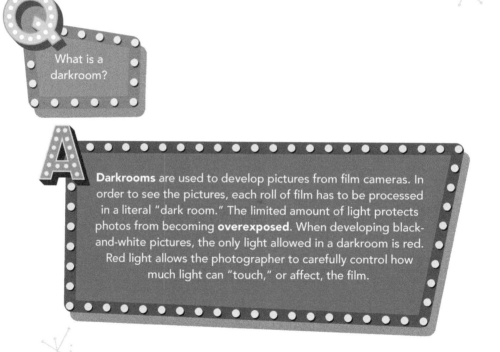

What is a darkroom?

Darkrooms are used to develop pictures from film cameras. In order to see the pictures, each roll of film has to be processed in a literal "dark room." The limited amount of light protects photos from becoming **overexposed**. When developing black-and-white pictures, the only light allowed in a darkroom is red. Red light allows the photographer to carefully control how much light can "touch," or affect, the film.

1. seln   — — — — —

2. vfiiwnedr   — — — — — — — — —

3. ybod   — — — —

4. tusehtr lseeare   — — — — — — — — — — — — — —

5. traperue   — — — — — — — —

6. eagmi nsseor   — — — — — — — — — — —

7. yommre drac   — — — — — — — — — —

8. dlc eenrsc   — — — — — — — — —

9. lahfs   — — — — —

10. rsue tsroncol   — — — — — — — — — — — —

11. aamrec   — — — — — —

12. tstruhe   — — — — — — —

13. mlfi   — — — —

14. socuf   — — — — —

15. cooltsnr   — — — — — — — —

16. ayettbr   — — — — — — —

17. dptori   — — — — — —

18. reopw   — — — — —

19. elsf rmeti   — — — — — — — — —

20. dre yee necudtroi   — — — — — — — — — — — — — — — —

— — — — — — — — — — —

 # BURST MODE

You are a photographer who loves to take pictures of things in action. Because you are always taking action shots, you typically use "burst mode" on your camera. Burst mode allows you to take several pictures together, one right after the other. This function is used to catch something moving at a high speed, like a person running or playing a ball game.

DIRECTIONS: You took a series of photos in burst mode, but when you tried to develop your pictures, you scrambled them. Put the pictures back in the right order using the number box in the top right corner of the game.

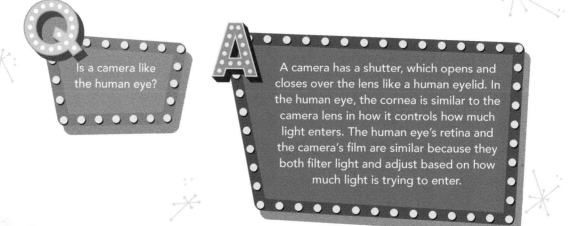

Q Is a camera like the human eye?

A A camera has a shutter, which opens and closes over the lens like a human eyelid. In the human eye, the cornea is similar to the camera lens in how it controls how much light enters. The human eye's retina and the camera's film are similar because they both filter light and adjust based on how much light is trying to enter.

DOROTHEA LANGE is a photographer who is best known for her work during the Great Depression. Her photo *Migrant Mother* is one of the most recognized pictures ever taken. The photo shows a mother and her two children, who were living in a **migrant** camp. The family was struggling to find food because the farm's crops had frozen and there was no work to make money. Dorothea, who was working for the Farm Security Administration (FSA) at the time, submitted the picture to the authorities. Because of the picture, the U.S. government sent food to the camp and helped the struggling families. One of the amazing things about art is that it can make a difference in people's lives.

SPEECH BUBBLES

Each scene in a graphic novel features many different pictures, but it also relies on words to help tell the story.

DIRECTIONS: Using the word bank below, fill in the word balloon or caption box with the word that best fits the action taking place in the square.

SOMEONE'S IN DANGER!

AHHH! HELP ME!

YOU ARE SAFE NOW.

I'LL KEEP THIS TOWN *SAFE!*

RIIIPP!

HERE I COME!

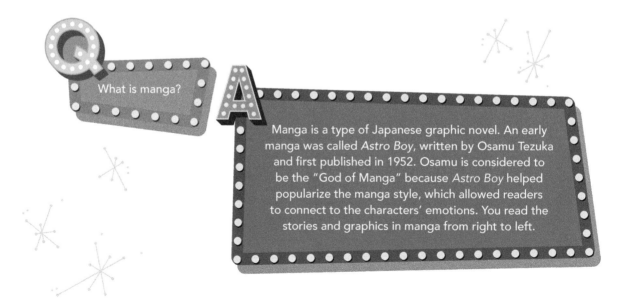

Q: What is manga?

A: Manga is a type of Japanese graphic novel. An early manga was called *Astro Boy*, written by Osamu Tezuka and first published in 1952. Osamu is considered to be the "God of Manga" because *Astro Boy* helped popularize the manga style, which allowed readers to connect to the characters' emotions. You read the stories and graphics in manga from right to left.

BURGER JOINT

What kind of burger do you like? Chances are, it's a little bit different from what your friends and family members prefer to eat. We're all unique—even when it comes to burgers!

DIRECTIONS: Build the perfect burger for each guest. Make sure to listen to their needs to create what they love. (Note: There is more than one right answer for each person.)

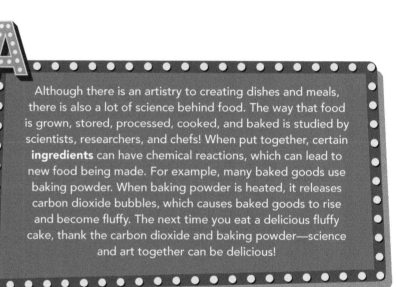

Q How is food both artistic and scientific?

A Although there is an artistry to creating dishes and meals, there is also a lot of science behind food. The way that food is grown, stored, processed, cooked, and baked is studied by scientists, researchers, and chefs! When put together, certain **ingredients** can have chemical reactions, which can lead to new food being made. For example, many baked goods use baking powder. When baking powder is heated, it releases carbon dioxide bubbles, which causes baked goods to rise and become fluffy. The next time you eat a delicious fluffy cake, thank the carbon dioxide and baking powder—science and art together can be delicious!

AWESOME ARTIST

CHARLES MICHEL is a French-Colombian culinary artist. This means he creates art by using food. Charles combines science, food, and art to create culinary designs that are appealing to the human mind. His goal is to create a food experience that **accentuates** the beauty of food and how it affects humans as they eat it.

Charles is a great example of a chef who explores the science behind the culinary arts.

NIGHT AT THE  MUSEUM

There are many famous sculptures that were created by artists throughout history.
Ten of them are hidden in the picture.

DIRECTIONS: Use the sculpture names provided below to find the right
10 sculptures in the picture on the right

> 1. Great Sphinx of Giza   2. *Christ the Redeemer*   3. *The Thinker*
> 4. Statue of Liberty   5. *Venus de Milo*   6. *David*   7. *Discobolus*
> 8. Bust of Nefertiti   9. Terracotta Warrior   10. Mount Rushmore

Q How do you make a sculpture?

A Making a sculpture can be tricky. Here are a few tips to get started! Draw the sculpture first. Have a plan! Next, build a base and create an **armature**, which is a sculpture-support system. Add material to your sculpture bit by bit. (One material used to create a sculpture is polymer clay.) Then add the details. If your sculpture is of a person, this means adding eyes and a nose. After that, **cure** your sculpture so it hardens. This means baking your sculpture at a high temperature. Decorate your art by painting it or adding other textures. Then display and admire your hard work!

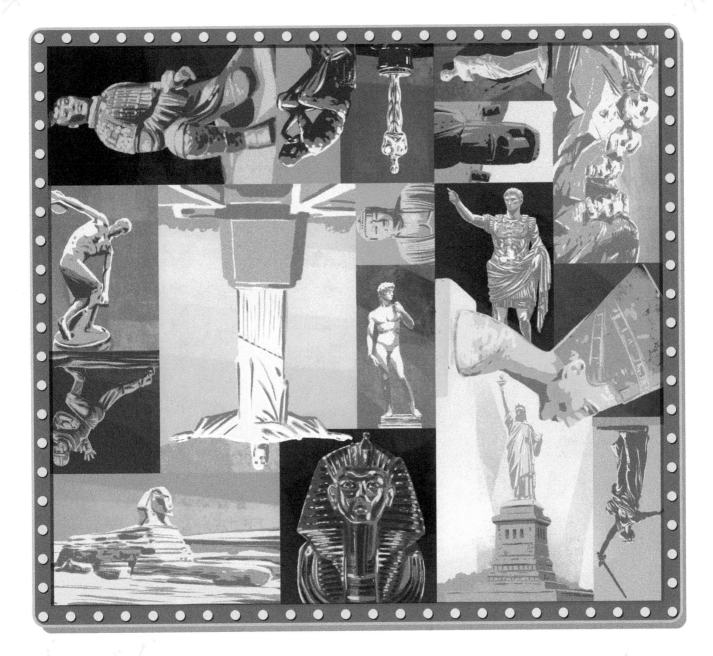

YOUR OWN  TREE FORT

You are an architect who has been hired to build a tree fort. Using the grid as a guide, build a tree house between the two trees.

DIRECTIONS: Decide what size materials to use based on the **dimensions** of the trees. Your tree house should include a floor, two visible sides, a roof, and a ladder that descends from the middle of the floor. Note: You can't cut off any branches or disrupt the leaves, so make sure your materials are the right size! You may use each material more than once.

BIRD'S-EYE

DIRECTIONS: Compare the two pictures of cityscapes. Do you see anything different between them? Look for 12 differences, circling them as you go.

FIND THE PAINTING THIEF!

DIRECTIONS: The *Mona Lisa* has gone missing! Help the museum curators find the real *Mona Lisa* painting in the crowd.

A A few reasons! The painting was part of France's King Francis I's royal collection and then owned by Napoleon. Also, in the early 1900s, the painting was stolen and wasn't found for two years. The person who sat for the portrait has never been identified—it remains a mystery! Today, you can see the *Mona Lisa* in the Louvre Museum in Paris.

A GRAND PLAY

You are a **choreographer** who loves to see actors use the whole auditorium, not just the stage. You are choreographing the play's most important scene and need to figure out how to get the actor from stage right to his spot at the X on the stage.

DIRECTIONS: Use the maze to get the actor there!

WHAT DID ONE ACTOR SAY TO ANOTHER ACTOR?

DIRECTIONS: Complete the crossword to learn new acting words. Maybe someday you'll use them when you're in a movie or onstage!

ACROSS

1. In a theater, a raised platform where actors perform
2. Main character who solves the problem
3. An emotional or exciting performance
4. A person whose profession is to pretend and deliver lines as a character
5. The text an actor reads
6. A funny performance

DOWN

7. A person who writes music
8. Hand and body movements that actors use to help deliver lines
9. The person who oversees and supervises the performances, actors, set, and crew
10. Works against the protagonist, and can be a person or a force
11. The person who creates the actors' steps in a performance
12. A person in a play or story
13. A segment of time in a performance
14. A performance that involves singing and dancing

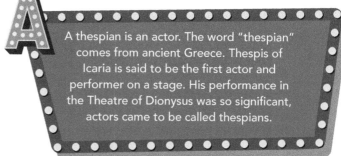

Q What is a thespian?

A A thespian is an actor. The word "thespian" comes from ancient Greece. Thespis of Icaria is said to be the first actor and performer on a stage. His performance in the Theatre of Dionysus was so significant, actors came to be called thespians.

actor	choreographer	drama	protagonist
antagonist	comedy	gesture	scene
character	composer	lines	stage
	director	musical	

STOP-MOTION... ACTION!

Stop-motion is a type of animation that was developed in the early 1900s. With stop-motion, you move objects slightly and take a picture after each move. When you put the pictures in order and display them rapidly, it looks like the object is moving, like in a movie! Have you ever tried to make a stop-motion movie?

DIRECTIONS: You are a cinematographer creating a stop-motion film. Choose the correct pictures to fill in the logical sequence.

Q What is a frame?

A In photography and film, "frame" means what is seen through the lens of a camera in a single shot. The frame can include people, scenery, and objects. It's important for actors to know what the frame is so they can move while acting and not be cut off by the frame of the camera. If an actor walks out of the frame by accident, the scene will have to be reshot. There are different types of angles that camera operators use to frame the shot, such as master, wide master, over-the-shoulder, and close-up. A **master/wide master** shows all actors in the scene. An **over-the-shoulder** shot is when the camera is positioned to film over an actor's shoulder, typically during dialogue. A **close-up** is when the camera frames the actor's face.

ERIC CARLE is an artist who is best known for his work in children's literature. Have you ever read the picture book *The Very Hungry Caterpillar*? The answer is likely yes, as 38 million copies of it have been sold! Eric has a distinct technique when creating the art for his stories. He makes collages by first painting tissue paper, then ripping it and placing it in patterns.

He encourages children to create collage art, and he receives hundreds of letters from them every week!

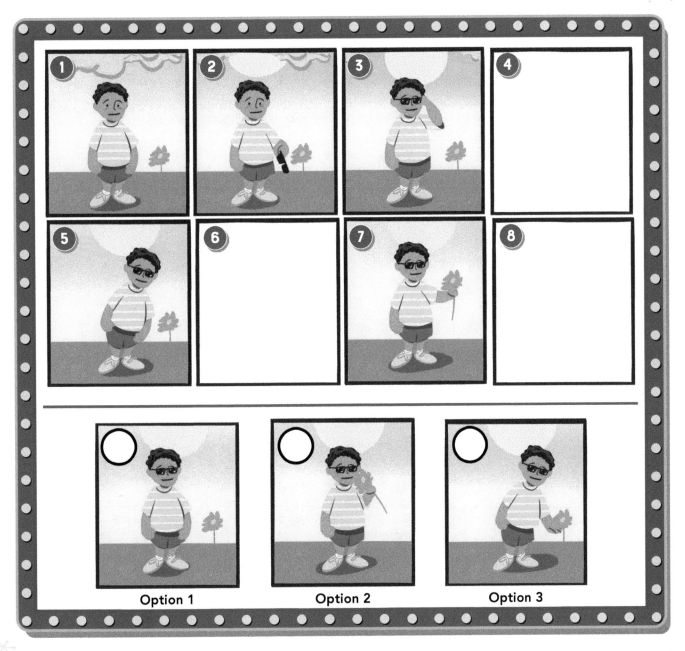

Option 1   Option 2   Option 3

GLASS PUZZLE

Stained-glass windows are built by arranging small pieces of colored glass in patterns and pictures, almost as if they are puzzle pieces that fit perfectly together. You are an artist who has been hired to create a stained-glass window for a building. You are almost finished creating the window when you realize five pieces are missing!

DIRECTIONS: Finish the window by figuring out where each stained-glass piece fits. Look carefully! There are more pieces than you need.

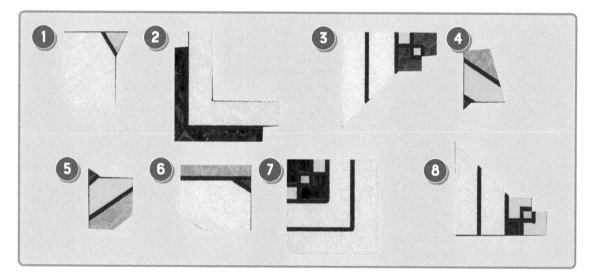

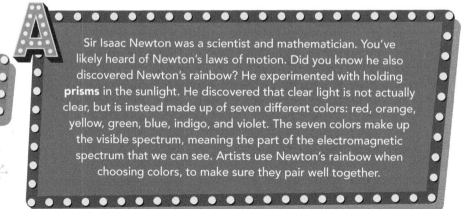

What is Newton's rainbow?

Sir Isaac Newton was a scientist and mathematician. You've likely heard of Newton's laws of motion. Did you know he also discovered Newton's rainbow? He experimented with holding **prisms** in the sunlight. He discovered that clear light is not actually clear, but is instead made up of seven different colors: red, orange, yellow, green, blue, indigo, and violet. The seven colors make up the visible spectrum, meaning the part of the electromagnetic spectrum that we can see. Artists use Newton's rainbow when choosing colors, to make sure they pair well together.

FOLLOW THE PATTERN

Mosaics are decorative artworks created by inlaying small pieces of multicolored materials together. They are typically made by arranging tile, glass, or stone into patterns. Observe the patterns of the mosaics below. What picture should come next in the sequences?

DIRECTIONS: Draw your answers in the empty spaces.

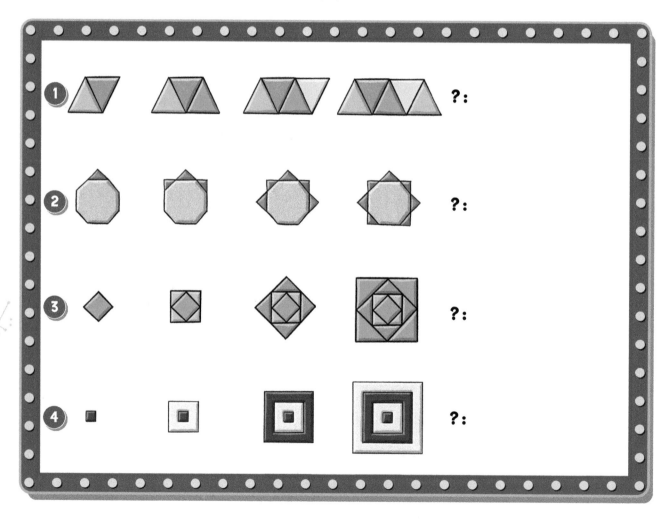

SECTION 5
MATH

THE SOPHIE GERMAIN CHALLENGE

Sophie Germain was a French mathematician born in 1776. During that time, girls were **discouraged** from studying math, but she fell in love with numbers. Against her parents' wishes, Sophie would hide under the covers and teach herself math. She even had a secret stash of candles that she would use to illuminate her books! Throughout her career, Sophie often used a **pseudonym**, a fake name, to submit her work. This was because many people refused to publish a woman's findings. (She would show *them*!)

This section is named after Sophie because her studies contributed greatly to the theory of elasticity and number theory, areas of mathematics that focus on the relationship between numbers. Even though she faced prejudice in a male-dominated career path, she never gave up. Her determination positively changed mathematics forever.

Today, math can be found everywhere we go—when we are shopping, cooking, or playing sports, and even in nature. Here you will face many different types of fun and challenging math problems—you might even be surprised that some of them are considered to be math. This section will help you discover how mathematics surrounds us.

 # MATH CLUES ALL AROUND US

Math vocabulary helps us solve many problems. Why? Mathematical words tell us what type of problem we are trying to solve, and how to solve it. You can think of math vocabulary as a clue!

DIRECTIONS: Find the words in the puzzle to get to know some common math terms.

algorithm	denominator	formula	operation	remainder
area	equation	fraction	perimeter	sequence
axis	expression	multiple	product	sum
coordinate	factor	numerator	quotient	unit

Who is the "Father of Math"?

Archimedes, a Greek mathematician, was nicknamed the "Father of Math" because he discovered the relationship between volume and the surface area of a sphere.

```
G H T O N O I S S E R P X E F R A H C Y
J R E A L G O R I T H M I W D R U O T R
M J K F E H E I W X O F I T E J O E I U
U F F F H R E D N I A M E R M R T D R E
L O E A O O R F U Y G S H B D E H F B E
T K Y R C F T Q A S H E H I S D R S D Q
I O S U D T A X I S Y J N E E F F B F U
P U S U C H O E B E R A O U Q J O F J A
L N C U M G O R T S T E F H U E R D K T
E O B R E F N J T E E T H H E I M B D I
T I J Y G P R O D U C T E D N P U F E O
O T R A H T K O T U N O Y U C J L J G N
O C U E U Y I I T I F J T I E Q A J F K
R A K R P O N M B H R E Y P O U I E N T
R R F A T U F H N R E T E M I R E P L E
E F U D J R K F J F E E R U I K J U E A
G Q P O I Y S D F K Y Q W Z M P O G L J
D N U M E R A T O R U T N E I T O U Q F
R O T A N I M O N E D E F O Y U R O W D
K E V U Q P H O H E G O P E R A T I O N
```

BREAKFAST FOR

You are hosting a party for 12 people who love breakfast food (including yourself), and everyone has a large appetite. You must go food shopping for all the ingredients you need.

DIRECTIONS: Look at the recipes then the art on the next page, and determine what to buy at the grocery store to make sure that every guest has one serving of *each* recipe. Happy shopping!

SCRAMBLED EGGS

Ingredients:
12 eggs
1½ cups cheese
½ cup milk
Serves: 6 people

BREAKFAST SANDWICHES

Ingredients:
1 egg
1 bagel
1 slice of bacon
¼ cup cheese
Serves: 1 person

FRENCH TOAST

Ingredients:
6 eggs
6 Tbsp butter
¼ cup milk
2 tsp cinnamon
12 slices of bread
Serves: 4 people

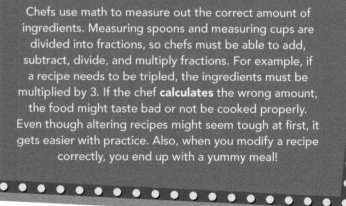

Q How do chefs use math?

A Chefs use math to measure out the correct amount of ingredients. Measuring spoons and measuring cups are divided into fractions, so chefs must be able to add, subtract, divide, and multiply fractions. For example, if a recipe needs to be tripled, the ingredients must be multiplied by 3. If the chef **calculates** the wrong amount, the food might taste bad or not be cooked properly. Even though altering recipes might seem tough at first, it gets easier with practice. Also, when you modify a recipe correctly, you end up with a yummy meal!

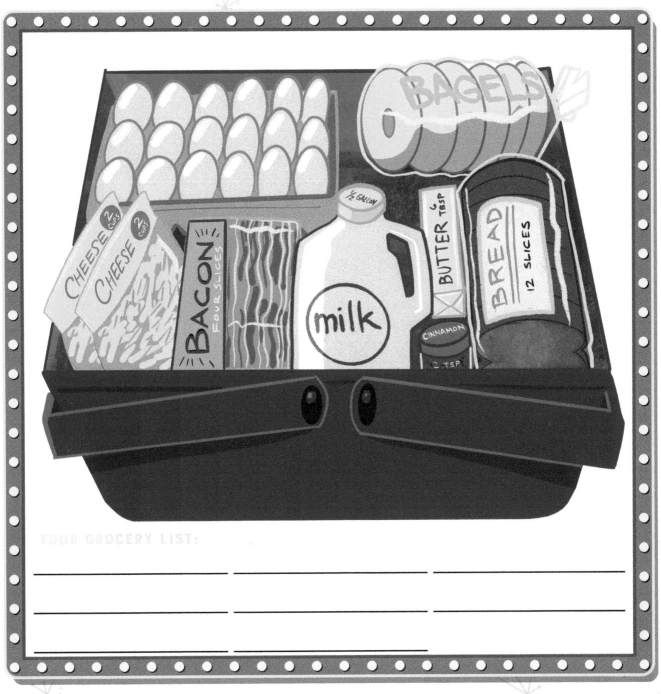

YOUR GROCERY LIST:

_____   _____   _____

_____   _____   _____

MAJOR  ITEMS

You are a manager at a grocery store. You are having a major sale and need to sort the items based on their sale percentage.

DIRECTIONS: Sort the grocery items into the correct shopping cart, depending on the amount it is discounted. For example, if bananas are originally $8.00 and their sale price is $4.00, bananas belong in the 50%-off cart. Draw an arrow from each item into the sale cart where it belongs. You can choose between the 25%-, 50%-, and 75%-off carts.

Q If you start with a penny and double the amount every day, how much will you have in one month?

A You will have $10,737,418.24 after 31 days!

HERE'S THE PROOF:

Day 1 $0.01	**Day 9** $2.56	**Day 17** $655.36	**Day 25** $167,772.16
Day 2 $0.02	**Day 10** $5.12	**Day 18** $1,310.72	**Day 26** $335,544.32
Day 3 $0.04	**Day 11** $10.24	**Day 19** $2,621.44	**Day 27** $671,088.64
Day 4 $0.08	**Day 12** $20.48	**Day 20** $5,242.88	**Day 28** $1,342,177.28
Day 5 $0.16	**Day 13** $40.96	**Day 21** $10,485.76	**Day 29** $2,684,354.56
Day 6 $0.32	**Day 14** $81.92	**Day 22** $20,971.52	**Day 30** $5,368,709.12
Day 7 $0.64	**Day 15** $163.84	**Day 23** $41,943.04	**Day 31** $10,737,418.24
Day 8 $1.28	**Day 16** $327.68	**Day 24** $83,886.08	

SHOPPING

Congrats! You just won a shopping spree! You have a $500 gift card to use at the mall.

DIRECTIONS: What ten items can you buy with your gift card?

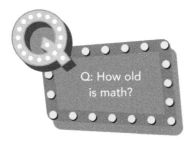

Q: How old is math?

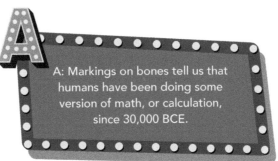

A: Markings on bones tell us that humans have been doing some version of math, or calculation, since 30,000 BCE.

DANICA McKELLAR is an actress and a mathematician. In addition to playing Winnie on *The Wonder Years* television show, she coauthored a **groundbreaking** mathematical physics theorem!

Danica has also written several books about math to help encourage and empower kids of all ages to pursue math. She wants to help kids discover that math is fun!

SUDOKU FOR YOU!

Sudoku is a great way to keep your brain's memory healthy. It's also a fun way to practice logic.

DIRECTIONS: Fill in the missing numbers, making sure you have numbers 1 to 9 in each box. You can only use numbers 1 to 9, and a number must be listed exactly once in each square, row, or column.

What does "sudoku" mean?

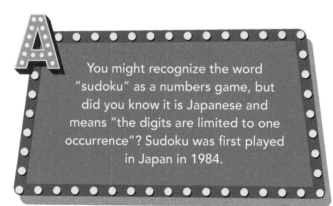

You might recognize the word "sudoku" as a numbers game, but did you know it is Japanese and means "the digits are limited to one occurrence"? Sudoku was first played in Japan in 1984.

	4		3		7	2	8	
3	8	9		2			4	6
	7		4			1	5	
		3	6	9	2	5		
		6		4	1		3	2
9				3			1	4
2		1	8	7				5
5			2		3	8		7
7		8	9	5				

READY, SET, SWIM!

DIRECTIONS: You are the coach of a swim team. At practice, you are conducting a workout called "staggered starts." Each swimmer will start one second after the person in front of them, beginning with Lane 1. As the coach, you must figure out who swam the fastest 50-meter freestyle. Look in the pool for each lane's finish time to help you determine the answer. Hint: If the swimmer in Lane 1 started at 0:00, then the swimmer in Lane 2 started at 0:01.

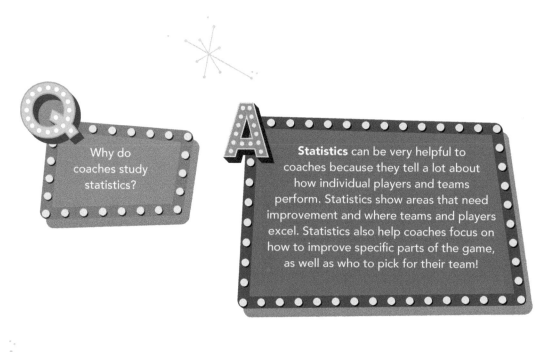

Q Why do coaches study statistics?

A **Statistics** can be very helpful to coaches because they tell a lot about how individual players and teams perform. Statistics show areas that need improvement and where teams and players excel. Statistics also help coaches focus on how to improve specific parts of the game, as well as who to pick for their team!

Did you know that billiards players use math to help them get the correct pool balls into the pockets?

DIRECTIONS: Solve the cryptogram to learn what specific area of math billiards players use.

Q Why do some sports require players to wear a number?

A Many sports require players to wear numbers. A few examples are soccer, football, and baseball. The players are identified by their numbers. This also makes it easy for fans to cheer on their favorite players: "Go, number twelve!" The practice of players wearing numbers has been traced back to Australia, where it is believed that numbers were first worn during soccer games.

JACOB BARNETT was born in 1998 and is the world's youngest astrophysics researcher. Jacob has autism, and doctors worried that he would never speak. But by age three, he could speak in four languages! He even taught himself calculus, **geometry**, and algebra in just two weeks! At age nine, he expanded Einstein's theory of relativity while he was playing with blocks.

To encourage others, he said, "In order to succeed, you have to look at everything with your own unique perspective."

What area of math do billiards players typically use?

A	B	C	D	E	F	G	H	I	J	K	L	M	N	O	P	Q	R	S	T	U	V	W	X	Y	Z
				12		1						19												6	

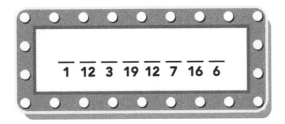

$$\overline{1}\ \overline{12}\ \overline{3}\ \overline{19}\ \overline{12}\ \overline{7}\ \overline{16}\ \overline{6}$$

SEEING DOUBLE

So much about math involves symmetry, or the exact correspondence between two different things.

DIRECTIONS: Connect each math symbol to its matching twin by drawing a line in the boxes between them. Make sure to not cross any paths!

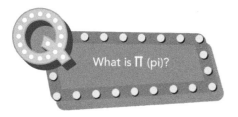

What is π (pi)?

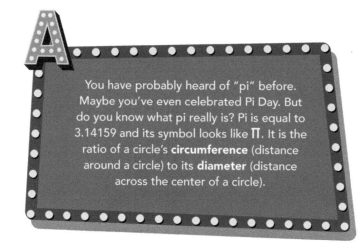

You have probably heard of "pi" before. Maybe you've even celebrated Pi Day. But do you know what pi really is? Pi is equal to 3.14159 and its symbol looks like π. It is the ratio of a circle's **circumference** (distance around a circle) to its **diameter** (distance across the center of a circle).

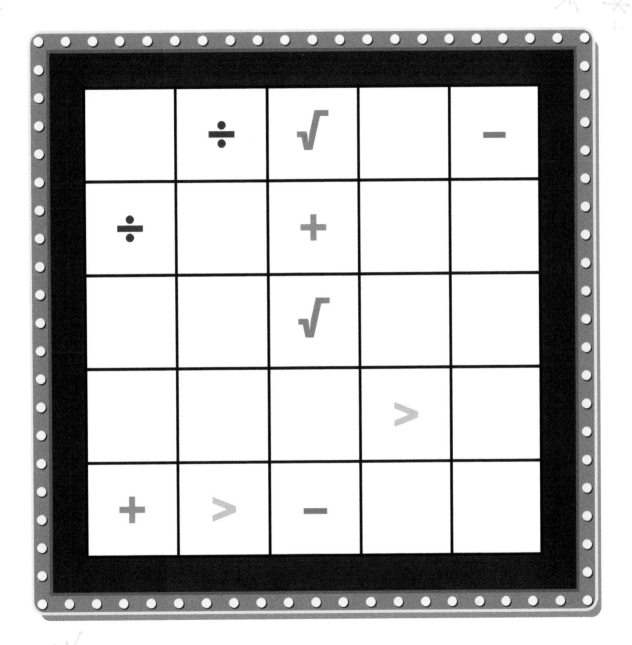

HIDDEN SHAPES AT THE

Did you know there are shapes everywhere you go? You can even find shapes at the beach!

DIRECTIONS: Find the: **triangles**, **circles**, **squares**, **rectangles**, **stars**, **rhombuses**, **octagons**, and **ovals** in the beach scene. Some shapes appear multiple times. There are over 60 shapes in the beach scene.

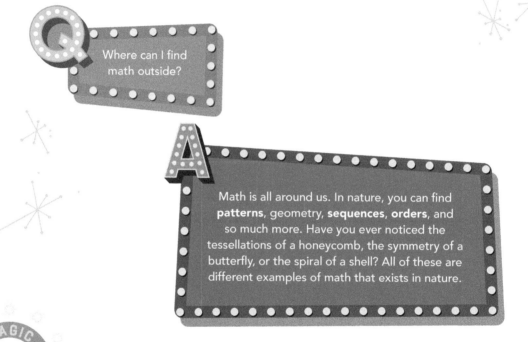

Where can I find math outside?

Math is all around us. In nature, you can find **patterns**, geometry, **sequences**, **orders**, and so much more. Have you ever noticed the tessellations of a honeycomb, the symmetry of a butterfly, or the spiral of a shell? All of these are different examples of math that exists in nature.

PAUL ERDÓS was a Hungarian mathematician who published over 1,500 math articles on various topics, such as math theories, math analytics, and geometry. He visited mathematicians all over the United States and Europe to discuss math and solve problems, traveling to more than 25 countries to do math.

Known for his eccentric personality, Paul believed if you were not doing math, than you simply were not alive. He took his area of expertise seriously!

Mathdoku is a challenging game of logic and trial and error. Traditionally, it has no instructions, but here are a few hints to help you. The connected squares follow the rule of the math symbol in the top left corner. The number next to the symbol is the total. For example, look at the two purple boxes that are connected with the 3+ in the corner. This means that by using only numbers 1, 2, 3, or 4, these two boxes must add up to equal 3.

DIRECTIONS: Solve the Mathdoku problem by making sure the numbers 1, 2, 3, and 4 appear one time in each column and row. Good luck—and remember that trial and error is a great way to solve problems!

What is Mathdoku?

Mathdoku, also known as KenKen, was invented by a Japanese educator named Tetsuya Miyamoto. The game intentionally has no instructions, as the inventor hoped it would inspire students to be self-motivated and learn without having to be told how to do it. Mathdoku helps train the brain to cleverly problem-solve. Without instructions, players must force their brains to focus and think hard about solving the game.

MAPPING YOUR

You and your friend are building a backyard garden so that you can grow your own vegetables. Your friend started planning where some of the garden goodies will go, but they can't seem to figure out where to place the rest.

DIRECTIONS: Use the garden blocks and the grid below to help your friend place all of the remaining crops, flowers, and the walkway. Pay close attention to the dimension of the garden goodies because they all fit perfectly together, like puzzle pieces. Keep in mind that you cannot cut or change the shape of any garden item. There's only one answer!

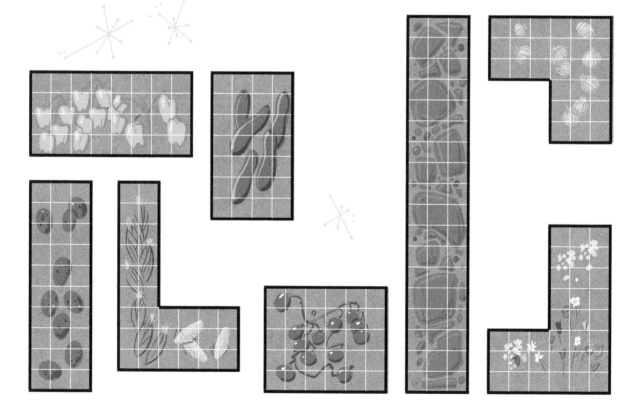

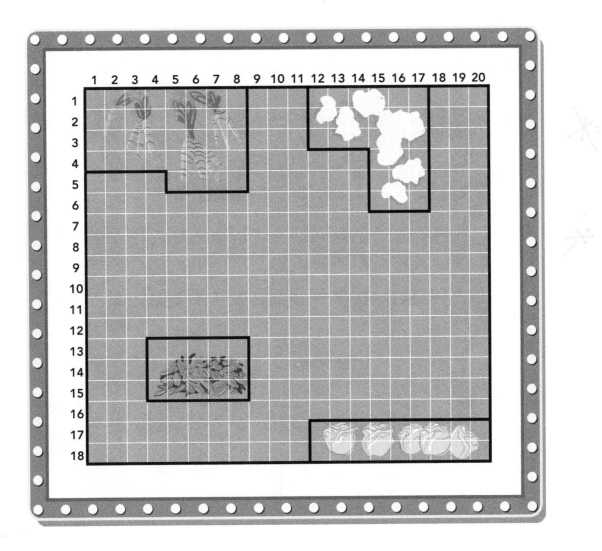

FACTOR PUZZLE

Factor puzzles are a fun way to problem-solve using multiplication. When multiplied, factors (the numbers on the lines outside each box) get you the number inside that box. To solve for the missing number in the empty square, you must first figure out which factors multiply to equal the numbers inside each box. To do this, you must look at the numbers in a row and think of a number that could divide both numbers. When you think of that number, write it on the outside of the box, to the left of 32 and the right of 24. Then do the same for 24 and 27. The idea is that the "outside" numbers on the opposite row and column match. To find the missing number in the bottom left-hand box, multiply the two numbers on the outside of that box.

DIRECTIONS: Solve the factor puzzle below!

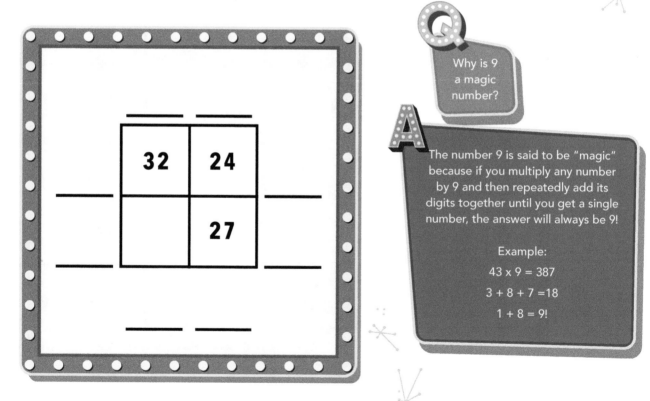

Why is 9 a magic number?

The number 9 is said to be "magic" because if you multiply any number by 9 and then repeatedly add its digits together until you get a single number, the answer will always be 9!

Example:
43 x 9 = 387
3 + 8 + 7 = 18
1 + 8 = 9!

DIRECTIONS: Connect each math symbol to its matching twin. Make sure to not cross any paths!

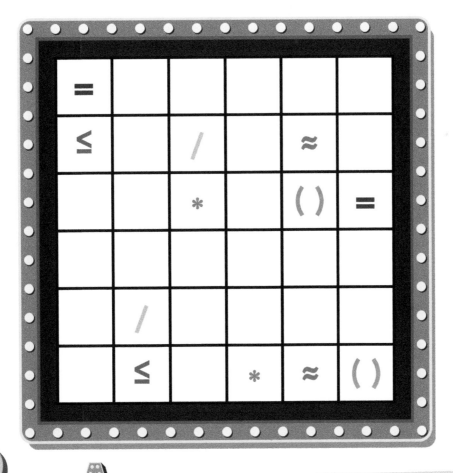

Q How much is infinity?

A Infinity is endless. It does not have an amount and cannot be measured because it is not a number like 1, 2, 3, and 4. Instead, it is considered a concept. An example of an infinite number is ⅓ as a decimal. ⅓ = 0.33333 (repeating). The repeating 3 in 0.33333 never ends. It will go on forever!

You solved the first Mathdoku—can you solve this one, too? Remember that traditional Mathdoku has no instructions, but here are a few hints to help you. The connected squares follow the rule of the math symbol in the top left corner. The number next to the symbol is the total.

DIRECTIONS: Solve the Mathdoku problem below. Good luck, and remember that trial and error is a great way to solve problems!

What is the largest number in the world?

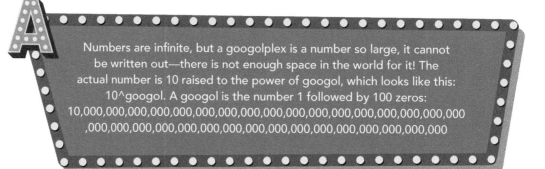

Numbers are infinite, but a googolplex is a number so large, it cannot be written out—there is not enough space in the world for it! The actual number is 10 raised to the power of googol, which looks like this: 10^{googol}. A googol is the number 1 followed by 100 zeros:
10,000,000,000,000,000,000,000,000,000,000,000,000,000,000,000,000
,000,000,000,000,000,000,000,000,000,000,000,000,000,000,000,000

CAN YOU FACTOR THE FINAL FACTOR?

You solved the first factor puzzle—can you solve this challenging one, too?

DIRECTIONS: Solve the factor puzzle below. Remember to find the missing number in the empty square. Use the outside lines to help you figure out which factor goes where!

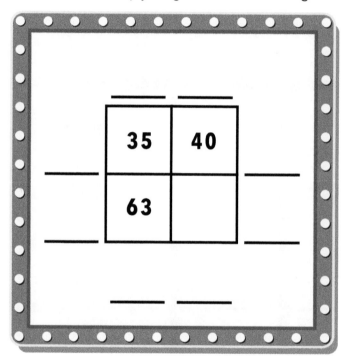

GLADYS WEST is a mathematician who was on the original team that developed the Global Positioning System (GPS). Taking into account forces of nature that affect our planet (such as gravity), Gladys programmed a computer to calculate the Earth's shape. The data that she calculated was ultimately used as the beginning foundation for GPS.

She loved gathering the data and working through the equations so much that she worked tirelessly day and night on the project. Her hard work **propelled** the project forward so quickly that its timeline was cut in half. The next time you use GPS, such as the map on your phone or in your family's car, you can thank Gladys West!

ANSWERS

SCIENCE: GAME 1

biologist—cells

marine biologist—fish

geologist—volcanoes

paleontologist—fossils

chemist—chemicals

botanist—plants

astronomer—stars

geneticist—DNA

meteorologist—weather

zoologist—animals

SCIENCE: GAME 2

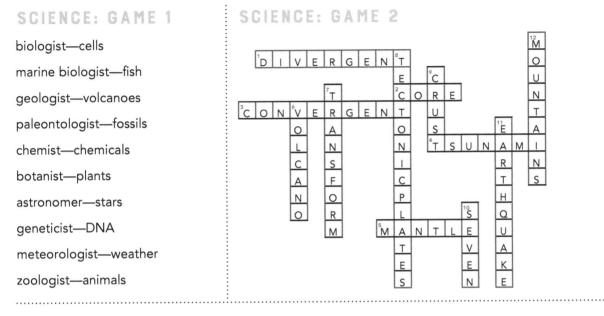

SCIENCE: GAME 3

Bags of sand and rocks are your two best options to help the town prevent flooding.
Both are heavy and can block water by disrupting the energy of the waves.

SCIENCE: GAME 4

SCIENCE: GAME 5

SCIENCE: GAME 6

HABITAT

BIODIVERSITY

CONSUMER

BIOLOGY

COMMUNITY

ECOLOGY

SPECIES

PRODUCER

DECOMPOSER

OXYGEN

ANIMALS

HERBIVORE

FUNGI

FOOD CHAIN

ECOLOGIST

SCIENCE: GAME 7

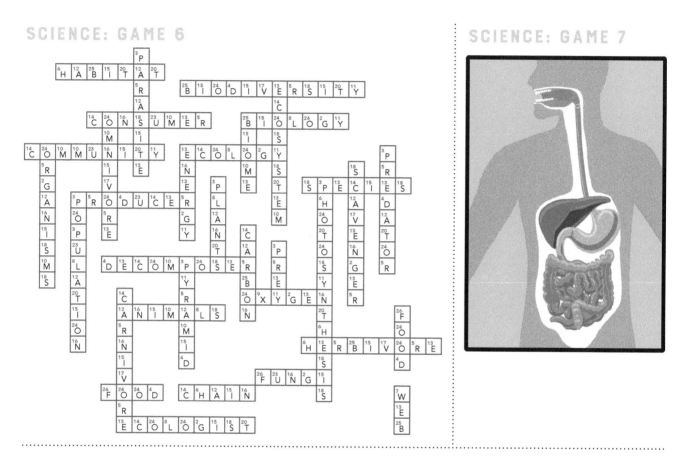

SCIENCE: GAME 8

llec nbaermem: cell membrane

cueunsl: nucleus

lclunouse: nucleolus

mpodnelisac ulucimret: endoplasmic reticulum

mosboesir: ribosomes

auoeclsv: vacuoles

dnmtoihcorin: mitochondrion

llec alwl: cell wall

ggloi tparapaus: Golgi apparatus

pstsaolrohcl: chloroplasts

mialna lelc: animal cell

ntpla lcel: plant cell

SCIENCE: GAME 9

```
C O N S T E L L A T I O N R E W F G H P
L R R F N M U M O E F R T G A L A X Y U
M F E P L A N E T A E R U O K L R E O T
R E A S R E A T Y R O E T E M M E A U J
F Q T M C T R H I O F I G T O B B F J K
H Y H O U E Q U I V R S U N O E R A O N
E H A S T R N U O E U E R H N A O U P E
Q I T P T A E T A R P H N I W E E E L W
X L M E E R A S T E R O I D S T L A A M
A O S W M A X R T M O Y C O N O J R N O
S A A Q O Y I F N M T X A W H O O T E O
T M T T C N S F L I M O L K L U N H R N
R E E K E E A L V J K E C L I P S E T L
O T L I A R U A E O J A M I E T Y L O P
N R L N R F R E E E L B S U O B B I G E
O E I L T G H O R B I T A B E R F T U L
M R T R R G G I B B L E E T A T O R U T
Y O E E V L O V E R A S E T U M N P O T
G O A E L M N R T S H O L T N B F E D R
R A L O S T H E R E R E H P S O M T A O
```

SCIENCE: GAME 10

SCIENCE: GAME 11

The leaves are blocking the solar panels from absorbing the sunlight. The clouds are blocking the sun from shining onto the solar panels. There is an electrical outlet that is not plugged in.

SCIENCE: GAME 12

Divya read the Celsius temperature and thought it was Fahrenheit, like back home. A 23-degree Fahrenheit day in Divya's hometown in the United States would indeed be very cold!

SCIENCE: GAME 13

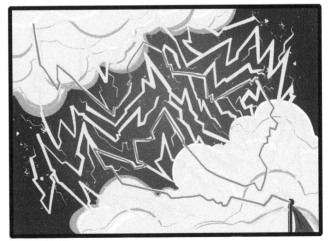

SCIENCE: GAME 14

The paper clip is the best option to close the circuit. Paper clips are made from metal, and metal is a conductor. Conductors allow electricity to flow through them.

SCIENCE: GAME 15

When you combine active dry yeast, water, dish soap, and hydrogen peroxide, you create a chemical reaction. The hydrogen peroxide breaks down into molecules: oxygen and water. The active dry yeast, when wet and added to the hydrogen peroxide, causes the hydrogen peroxide to separate faster. The dish soap traps the oxygen into bubbles, which creates the thick oozy substance we call Elephant Toothpaste.

TECHNOLOGY: GAME 16

1. 0, 0	5. 1
2. 0, 1	6. 1
3. 0, 0	7. 1, 0
4. 1, 1	8. 0, 0, 0, 0

TECHNOLOGY: GAME 17

HELLO

TECHNOLOGY: GAME 18

1. hard drive: diamond bending a hammer + steering wheel

2. webcam: spiderweb + camera

3. laptop: an arrow pointing to lap + spinning top

4. flash drive: an arrow pointing to camera flash + steering wheel

5. online: "on" lying on a line

6. virus: V + arrow pointing to eye's iris

7. database: bar graph picture + baseball base

8. download: an arrow pointing down + computer loading symbol

9. in-box: the word "in" inside a box

10. search engine: binoculars + engine

TECHNOLOGY: GAME 19

1. computer
2. data
3. storage
4. cloud
5. processor
6. upload
7. cyber

8. malware
9. software
10. download
11. Internet
12. World Wide Web
13. screen
14. code

15. digital
16. memory
17. system
18. desktop
19. laptop
20. network

Answer to star letters:
Computer Science

TECHNOLOGY: GAME 20

1. left, left
2. down, up, right
3. down
4. up, down
5. right, up

TECHNOLOGY: GAME 21

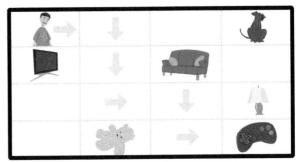

TECHNOLOGY: GAME 22

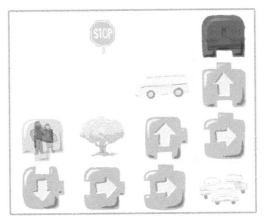

TECHNOLOGY: GAME 23

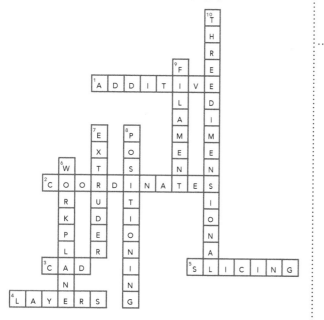

Crossword solution:
1. ADDITIVE
2. COORDINATES
3. CAD
4. LAYERS
5. SLICING
6. WORKPLANE
7. EXTRUDER
8. POSITIONING
9. FILAMENT
10. THREEDIMENSIONAL

TECHNOLOGY: GAME 24

You have died of dysentery!

TECHNOLOGY: GAME 25

```
E S T O B C E R T T P E L O S N O C A P
A D S H C H A R A C T E R S S T U B C I
T O O P S E R R C S E H E I R X I P H X
H L P C O A V A T A R J T M C O M P E E
E E T H M T T H I S T A R U L T C R A L
S R E Y A L P U O T O N O L C O N S T S
D M J N K U L P N J U I G A R C A D E S
A C O N T R O L L E R H A T E T U P O P
P Y Y J O Y A R E T M E M I E C I V E D
E I S O C I A L S H R T I O S H N G M E
M J T T U O M L T E X H N N O Y L R O V
A L I V I D E A Y E M L G T O R K A O E
G O C S T O G A M E P K S H H O H P L L
E R K D A P L B T L O M E E K M T H A O
D E M O T P A S R T U N N M O E D I V P
E D U C I G Y M J O Y P A D A M G C O E
D O N T E S R E M E M T H S S O O S I R
A P L O P E N E N D E D C H O I T E H S
R U S H N O I T C A E V I L R E M A G I
M C O L E D U C A T I O N A L O B M K T
```

TECHNOLOGY: GAME 26

TECHNOLOGY: GAME 27

1. ptaecudt: duct tape
2. daadbrcor: cardboard
3. ttliegr: glitter
4. aeeceipipnrs: pipe cleaners
5. ppiisssolecckt: Popsicle sticks
6. sroicsss: scissors
7. lsepcin: pencils
8. easslitc: elastics
9. sootl: tools
10. eulrr: ruler
11. geglurun: glue gun
12. ingrts: string
13. blylcaeescr: recyclables
14. skboo: books
15. ckbols: blocks
16. cafbri: fabric
17. ppoomms: pom-poms

TECHNOLOGY: GAME 28

1: printing press, 2: light bulb, 3: microwave, 4: refrigerator, 5: shoelaces, 6: telephone, 7: camera, 8: glasses, 9: radio, 10: car, 11: screw, 12: vacuum, 13: wheel, 14: pencil, 15: compass, 16: toilet, 17: calendar, 18: clock, 19: television, 20: pulley, 21: vaccines, 22: telescope, 23: train

TECHNOLOGY: GAME 29

low-tech:
pencil, buzzer, cardboard box, mirror, scissors, fork, pushpin, stapler, fly swatter, umbrella

high-tech:
robot, tablet, car, smartphone, camera, treadmill, game controller

TECHNOLOGY: GAME 30

Lightning 1 is connected to the orange kite. The orange kite is connected to Maceo.

Lightning 2 is connected to the blue kite. The blue kite is connected to Malik.

Lightning 3 is connected to the yellow kite. The yellow kite is connected to Nia.

Lightning 4 is connected to the red kite. The red kite is connected to Eddie.

Lightning 5 is connected to the green kite. The green kite is connected to Emma.

ENGINEERING: GAME 31

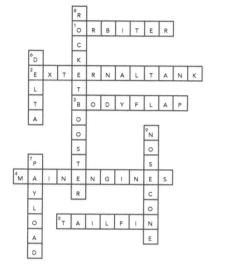

Across:
1. ORBITER
2. EXTERNAL TANK
3. BODY FLAP
4. MAIN ENGINES
5. TAIL FIN

Down:
6. DELTA
7. PAYLOAD
8. ROCKSTOOSTR
9. NOSE CONE

ENGINEERING: GAME 32

ENGINEERING: GAME 33

A	B	C	D	E	F	G	H	I	J	K	L	M
6	10	12	18	7	19	1	13	11	20	2	14	21

N	O	P	Q	R	S	T	U	V	W	X	Y	Z
23	3	25	15	4	16	22	5	17	8	24	9	26

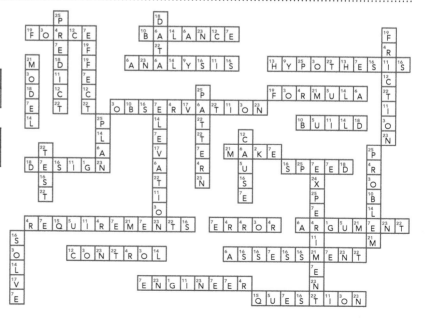

FORCE
BALANCE
ANALYSIS
HYPOTHESIS
FORMULA
OBSERVATION
BUILD
MAKE
SPEED
DESIGN
REQUIREMENTS
ERROR
ARGUMENT
CONTROL
ASSESSMENT
ENGINEER
QUESTION
SOLVE

ENGINEERING: GAME 34

- lever
- pulley
- wheel
- wedge
- plane
- screw

ENGINEERING: GAME 35

The bucket fits best into Step I because after the tennis ball enters the bucket, the weight of the tennis ball in the bucket will pull the pulley string down, turning the fan on and blowing the sailboat toward the hammer that will turn the switch off.

ENGINEERING: GAME 36

ENGINEERING: GAME 37

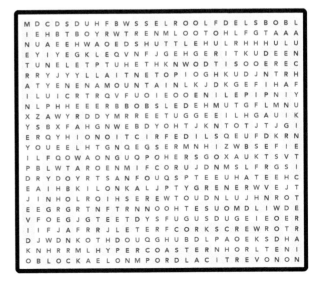

ENGINEERING: GAME 38

Aerospace engineer ⟶ Space shuttle

Agricultural engineer ⟶ Tractor

Civil engineer ⟶ Hard hat

Mechanical engineer ⟶ Gears

Biomedical engineer ⟶ Mechanical heart

Electrical engineer ⟶ Circuit board

Chemical engineer ⟶ Chemicals

Sound engineer ⟶ Soundboard

Robotic engineer ⟶ Robotic hand

Automotive engineer ⟶ Car engine

ENGINEERING: GAME 39

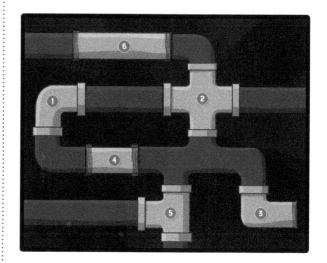

ENGINEERING: GAME 40

ENGINEERING: GAME 41

ENVIRONMENTAL__ENGINEERS__
SOLVE__ENVIRONMENTAL__PROBLEMS

ENGINEERING: GAME 42

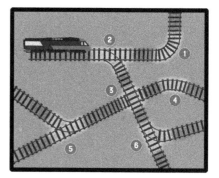

ENGINEERING: GAME 43

1. Suspension bridge
2. Drawbridge
3. Simple-suspension bridge
4. Cable-stayed bridge
5. Tilt bridge
6. Bridge/tunnel
7. Trestle bridge
8. Arch bridge
9. Cable-stayed suspension bridge

ENGINEERING: GAME 44

1: C

2: B

3: D

4: A

ENGINEERING: GAME 45

```
E R S L A B I N G B O W S T R I N G P Q
R A S B T L T Q U B R E A L M N O M A B
O S I L T M I N P L R O P V W P R A T T
M V C A B L E S T A Y E D S U S B E E O
I E R T T S D P A V N H D E E E H B F I
T R R T O R A A R C I T P L W R G O N B
L T T I L E R T R U S S T O O E W D F P
A I G C N M C A E P F R I I H O S T I A
B C A E U N H L I O A D N J W J K H N R
D A I N A V L Y S N N E P K E O K N K W
E L O O N R I O L T E E O S T C O I O M
R L H C R A I E Y O M N L U A I N D U T
E I A E T N P T O O R E S B S P O N E L
V F Q U L E E T S N T O L N P E R M E N
O T R O O R E U O N A E E L W A R D A P
C A E U E F F H K M M P Q U O R E O B R
E E N K E R U T N A S E A B N N M I N Q
R T R Q U R V B C U O F L O A T I N G U
T A W X O Y T P S L R E V E L I T N A C
P D E W A R R E N N B M C Z E G I J H O
```

ART: GAME 46

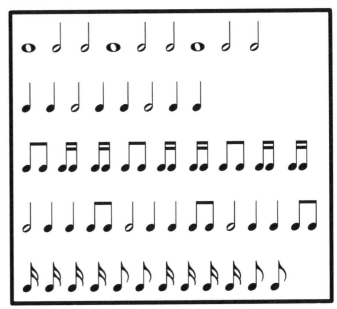

ART: GAME 47

```
T I M P A N I E R T S E H I A N T O M T
E G J D B D W Y R O L E A T H R O U E R
T U B A E R Y A I G U I R O E E R E J U
R E R G H Y T O N J C F M B G D T W S T
U D F F E I R A E H E A O O H I R V J E
M Q U O U T I S H D L R N E J K H C U N
P E T G B R G H O D L I I T S T D L E I
E O O M T G J E G H O O C D J R E A R L
T S O N F H D G O U M N A V N O G R F O
H A N R D E N O H P O L Y X E M Y I O D
A X A O G D O G E T U Y R U R B X N O N
R O B H P T N C L B S R C M S O Q E N A
M P E H J O T I M P A X C Y T N U T A M
T H U C G M N S F E E S V R M E U T L P
H O F N W T F L U T E Z S O N B M U H R
D N H E H K I E U L U D C O R G A L A S
E E D R D U K U L E L E X Y O R T L R C
H Y R F D V I O E O J N A B I N L O P J
O O R M O L E I P S N E K C O L G F L T
I L N I L O I V E G J G O N A I P E I E
```

ART: GAME 49

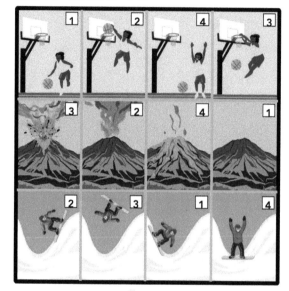

Answer to star letters: Photoshop

ART: GAME 48

1. l e n s
2. v i e w f i n d e r
3. b o d y
4. s h u t t e r   r e l e a s e
5. a p e r t u r e
6. i m a g e   s e n s o r
7. m e m o r y   c a r d
8. l c d   s c r e e n
9. f l a s h
10. u s e r   c o n t r o l s
11. c a m e r a
12. s h u t t e r
13. f i l m
14. f o c u s
15. c o n t r o l s
16. b a t t e r y
17. t r i p o d
18. p o w e r
19. s e l f - t i m e r
20. r e d - e y e   r e d u c t i o n

ART: GAME 50

1. ***Ahhh!*** Help me!
2. Someone's in danger!
3. ***Riiipp!***
4. Here I come!
5. You are safe now.
6. I'll keep this town ***safe***!

ART: GAME 51

Beau's burger: beef patty, bacon, pepper jack cheese

Lee's burger: bun, veggie burger, pepper jack cheese, sweet relish, lettuce, tomatoes, American cheese

Lani's burger: bun, beef patty, bacon, pepper jack cheese, sweet relish, chicken patty, American cheese

Effie's burger: chicken patty, bun, sweet relish, lettuce, tomatoes

TJ's burger: lettuce, tomatoes

ART: GAME 52

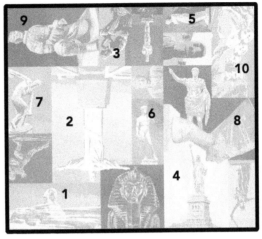

1. Great Sphinx of Giza
2. *Christ the Redeemer*
3. *The Thinker*
4. Statue of Liberty
5. *Venus de Milo*
6. *David*
7. *Discobolus*
8. Bust of Nefertiti
9. Terracotta Warrior
10. Mount Rushmore

ART: GAME 53

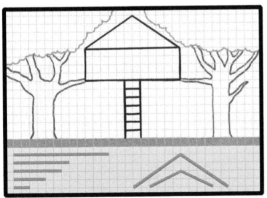

ART: GAME 54

ART: GAME 55

ART: GAME 56

ART: GAME 57

ART: GAME 58

Pic 4: Option 1

Pic 6: Option 3

Pic 8: Option 2

ART: GAME 59

ART: GAME 60

1.

2.

3.

4.

MATH: GAME 61

```
G H T O N O I S S E R P X E F R A H C Y
J R E A L G O R I T H M I W D R U O T R
M J K F E H E I W X O F I T E J O E I U
U F F F H R E D N I A M E R M R T D R E
L O E A O O R F U Y G S H B D E H F B E
T K Y R C F T Q A S H E H I S D R S D Q
I O S U D T A X I S Y J N E E F F B F U
P U S U C H O E B E R A O U Q J O F J A
L N C U M G O R T S T E F H U E R D K T
E O B R E F N J T E E T H H E I M B D I
T I J Y G P R O D U C T E D N P U F E O
O T R A H T K O T U N O Y U C J L J G N
O C U E U Y I I T I F J T I E Q A J F K
R A K R P O N M B H R E Y P O U I E N T
R R F A T U F H N R E T E M I R E P L E
E F U D J R K F J F E E R U I K J U E A
G Q P O I Y S D F K Y Q W Z M P O G L J
D N U M E R A T O R U T N E I T O U Q F
R O T A N I M O N E D E F O Y U R O W D
K E V U Q P H O H E G O P E R A T I O N
```

MATH: GAME 62

Eggs: 54 eggs = 3 cartons

Cheese: 6 cups of cheese = 3 bags

Bagels: 12 bagels = 2 bags

Bacon: 12 pieces of bacon = 3 packages

Milk: 1 cup of milk = 1 carton

Butter: 18 Tbsp of butter = 3 sticks

Cinnamon: 6 tsp cinnamon = 3 shakers

Bread: 36 slices of bread = 3 bags

MATH: GAME 63

25% off: cookies, doughnuts, apples, flowers, pizza

50% off: ice cream, crackers, cereal, bananas

75% off: burger, juice box, salad

MATH: GAME 64

shirt, bag, doll, pants, chair, candy bar, bicycle, controller, disco ball, skateboard

(Everything but the hat.)

MATH: GAME 65

1	4	5	3	6	7	2	8	9
3	8	9	1	2	5	7	4	6
6	7	2	4	8	9	1	5	3
4	1	3	6	9	2	5	7	8
8	5	6	7	4	1	9	3	2
9	2	7	5	3	8	6	1	4
2	3	1	8	7	6	4	9	5
5	9	4	2	1	3	8	6	7
7	6	8	9	5	4	3	2	1

MATH: GAME 66

Lane 1 Start time: 00:00 Finish time: 00:32 Time swimming: 00:32

Lane 2 Start time: 00:01 Finish time: 00:29 Time swimming: 00:28

Lane 3 Start time: 00:02 Finish time: 00:30 Time swimming: 00:28

Lane 4 Start time: 00:03 Finish time: 00:28 Time swimming: 00:25 (winner)

Lane 5 Start time: 00:04 Finish time: 00:33 Time swimming: 00:29

Lane 6 Start time: 00:05 Finish time: 00:32 Time swimming: 00:27

MATH: GAME 67

Answer: GEOMETRY

A	B	C	D	E	F	G	H	I	J	K	L	M
				12		1						19

N	O	P	Q	R	S	T	U	V	W	X	Y	Z
	3			16		7					6	

MATH: GAME 68

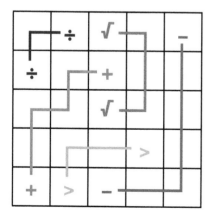

MATH: GAME 69

MATH: GAME 70

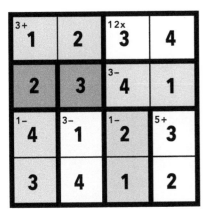

3+ 1	2	12x 3	4
2	3	3- 4	1
1- 4	3- 1	1- 2	5+ 3
3	4	1	2

MATH: GAME 71

MATH: GAME 72

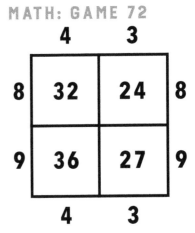

	4	3	
8	32	24	8
9	36	27	9
	4	3	

MATH: GAME 73

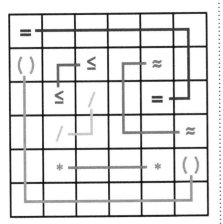

MATH: GAME 74

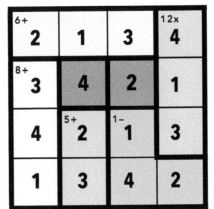

6+ 2	1	3	12x 4
8+ 3	4	2	1
4	5+ 2	1- 1	3
1	3	4	2

MATH: GAME 75

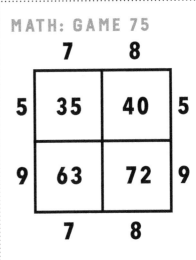

	7	8	
5	35	40	5
9	63	72	9
	7	8	

WHAT LEVEL  ARE YOU?

LEVEL 1: 5–215 POINTS

Congratulations for making it to the Smartypants level! You worked through the tough games and didn't give up! Now make sure to share with your friends or family how much of a STEAM Smartypants you are!

LEVEL 2: 216–430 POINTS

Congratulations for making it to the Prodigy level! The challenging games and questions could not fool you! You worked super hard strengthening your brain to become a Prodigy of STEAM. Be very proud of your smarts—tell a friend!

LEVEL 3: 431–645 POINTS

Congratulations for making it to the Brainiac level! You problem-solved, thought logically, and tried your best through all the games and questions. Make sure to tell your teacher how amazing you are!

LEVEL 4: 646–860 POINTS

Congratulations for making it to the Mastermind level! You persevered through the challenging games to become the ultimate Mastermind of STEAM! Go tell a friend how smart you are!

LEVEL 5: 861–1,095 POINTS

Congratulations for making it to the highest Genius level! You really *are* a Whiz Kid! You challenged your brain though all the games and worked so hard! Be very proud of yourself. Announce to a family member or friend that they are in the presence of a Genius!

GLOSSARY

A

ACCENTUATE: to make more noticeable

ADVOCATE: to support something, someone, or an idea

ALGORITHMS: sets of rules when calculating

ARMATURE: a sculpture support system

ARTIFICIAL INTELLIGENCE (AI): A type of computer science that uses machines that work, think, and react like humans

ATOMS: the building blocks of all matter

ATMOSPHERE: the mass of air surrounding Earth

ATRIUM: the chamber of the heart that receives blood from the veins

B

BINARY NUMBER: a 0 or a 1 used in the binary number system

BIT: a digit in the binary number system

BIOFUEL: fuel created from dead matter

BIOME: an ecological community

BOUNDARIES: in plate tectonics, the dividing lines or spaces between the plates

BLACK HOLE: a celestial field with a strong gravitational pull that light can't escape from

BRASS INSTRUMENTS: musical instruments that a musician blows into, vibrating their lips

BUDGET: a specific amount of money to be used for something

C

CALCULATE: to solve mathematically

CARDIOVASCULAR SYSTEM: the body system that circulates the blood

CHLOROPHYLL: the green pigment in plants

CHOREOGRAPHER: someone who arranges the steps for a performance

CIRCLE: a figure in which all points are equidistant from a center

CIRCUMFERENCE: the distance around a circle

CLOSE-UP SHOT: a film shot framing an actor's face

COMBINE: to put things together

COMPUTER-AIDED DESIGN (CAD): software that designs and creates 3-D–printed objects

CONSOLE: a special computer used to play video games

CONTRIBUTION: helpful and important information that is provided, especially to a field of study like science, technology, engineering, art, or math!

CONVERGENT PLATE BOUNDARIES: when tectonic plates move toward each other

COORDINATES: a set of values that shows a location

COSMOLOGY: the study of the development of the universe

CURE: to bake a sculpture at a high temperature to harden it

D

DARKROOM: a room with no light or a safelight for developing photographs

DECIDUOUS: shedding or falling off every year, as in leaves that fall from a tree

DIAMETER: distance across the center of a circle

DIMENSION: a measurement (usually length, width, height)

DISCOURAGED: to lose interest and enthusiasm

DIVERGENT PLATE BOUNDARIES: when tectonic plates move away from each other

DOCTORATE: the highest educational degree

DRAWBRIDGE: a kind of bridge with a hinge at one end so that it can be raised

E

ECOSYSTEM: a community of organisms and their environment functioning as a unit

EDUCATOR ASTRONAUTS: teach students and teachers about space exploration

ERODE: destroyed by wearing away

ERUPT: when a volcano becomes active and spews out lava and ash

F

FIRST LAW OF MOTION: Newton's first law of motion states that an object in motion stays in motion unless acted upon, and an object at rest will stay at rest unless acted upon

G

GEOMETRY: the branch of mathematics that deals with lines, angles, and solids

GRAVITATIONAL: the force or pull toward something

GROUNDBREAKING: innovative in creative thinking

H

HIGH TIDE: when water is at its greatest elevation

I

INGREDIENTS: the food that is combined to make a meal

IRRIGATION: artificial watering system for plants

L

LOW TIDE: when water is at its lowest elevation

M

MACHINE LEARNING (ML): A type of Artificial Intelligence whereby computers learn data and improve themselves based on that data

MAKERSPACE: a collaborative work space where people create things

MAMMALS: warm-blooded higher-vertebrates (including humans) that feed their young with secreted milk and that have skin covered by varying degrees of hair

MASTER OR WIDE MASTER SHOT: a film shot that shows all actors in a scene

MIGRANT: a person who moves from one place to another, typically looking for work

MISSION SPECIALISTS: astronauts who conduct research on a space mission, control robotics, and go on spacewalks

MONORAIL: a train that travels on one rail instead of two

MOSAIC: decoration made by inlaying small pieces of multicolored materials

O

OCTAGON: a plane figure with eight straight sides and eight angles

ORDER: arrangement of objects in a particular way

OSSIFIES: turns to bone

OVEREXPOSED: having exposed a photograph to too much light in the developing process

OVAL: having a rounded and slightly elongated outline or shape like that of an egg

OVER-THE-SHOULDER SHOT: a shot filmed from over an actor's shoulder

P

PARALLEL CIRCUIT: when electricity flows through two or more paths

PATENTED: legally protected under proprietary rights

PATTERN: how something is designed or appears in nature by way of repeating characteristics

PERCUSSION INSTRUMENTS: musical instruments that make their sound by being hit or shaken, causing vibration

PHOTOSYNTHESIS: the synthesis of chemical compounds with the help of radiant energy, particularly light

PHYSICS: the science of matter and energy and their interactions

PILOT ASTRONAUTS: fly a space shuttle and oversee a mission

PRESSURIZED: to have pressure

PRISM: glass or transparent geometric figure that refracts light

PROGRAMMING: the process of preparing a program for a device

PROPELLED: driven or pushed forward

PSEUDONYM: a fake name

R

RECTANGLE: a quadrilateral with four right angles

RHOMBUS: a parallelogram with opposite equal acute angles, opposite equal obtuse angles, and four equal sides

S

SCRATCH CODE: visual programming languages for simplifying the creation of games, music, and animation

SEQUENCES: continuous or connected series

SERIES CIRCUIT: when all components of a circuit are in a row

SIMPLE MACHINE: any mechanical device that applies force, like a lever or pulley

SOLAR PANEL: devices designed to absorb the sun's rays in order to generate electricity

SQUARE: a plane figure with four equal sides

STAR: a polygon with five points

STATISTICS: a set of data that you can draw a conclusion from

STRING INSTRUMENTS: musical instruments that make their sound from vibrating strings

T

TECTONIC PLATES: pieces of Earth's crust and uppermost mantle

TIDES: the rise and fall of water levels

TRANSFORM PLATE BOUNDARIES: when tectonic plates move past each other, side by side

TRANSPORT: to carry goods from one place to another

TRIANGLE: a polygon with three sides

U

UPPER MANTLE: the part of Earth just beneath its crust that is made up of rock that is fluid and can move

V

VOLCANIC ROCK: rock formed from lava erupted from a volcano

W

WOODWIND INSTRUMENTS: musical instruments that make their sound from vibrating air after being blown into

FURTHER EXPLORATION

Books, websites, and other resources with which parents and teachers can find more exciting mental challenges to stimulate their kids.

APPS:

LEGO Life—Love building with LEGO? Share building ideas and learn how to build amazing LEGO creations from other users.

Lightbot—Learn how to code with this super fun puzzle app that is perfect for beginner coders.

RollerCoaster Tycoon Touch—Build your own rollercoasters and theme parks in this app, just like real-life mechanical engineers!

Truss Me!—Learn how to build truss structures, such as bridges and cranes. Challenge your inner engineer with an app that was designed by a rocket scientist!!

BOOKS:

Brain Games: Big Book of Boredom Busters, by Stephanie Warren Drimmer and Gareth Moore

Challenging Puzzles for Smart Kids, by Terry Stickels

Difficult Riddles for Smart Kids, by M. Prefontaine

I Love Science: A Journal for Self-Discovery and Big Ideas, by Rachel Ignotofsky

STEM Doodle Book, by Sumita Mukherjee

STEM Activity Book, by Catherine Bruzzone, Sam Hutchinson, and Jenny Jacoby

MAGAZINES:

Ask: Arts & Sciences for Kids, Cricket Media

Muse, Cricket Media

Reinvented Magazine, Reinvented Inc.

TV SHOWS:

Bill Nye the Science Guy

The Magic School Bus

MythBusters Jr.

Project Mc2

SciGirls

The World According to Jeff Goldblum

WEBSITES:

Center for Game Science, centerforgamescience.org

Code, code.org

Khan Academy, khanacademy.org

Scratch, scratch.mit.edu

Tynker Coding for Kids, tynker.com

VIDEO GAMES:

Minecraft

The Oregon Trail

Tetris

FOR MORE INFORMATION ON STEAM LEADERS:

Black Pioneers of Science and Invention, by Louis Haber

Everyday Superheroes: Women in STEM Careers, by Erin Twamley and Joshua Sneideman

Have You Thanked an Inventor Today?, by Patrice McLaurin

Hidden Figures: The True Story of Four Black Women and the Space Race, by Margot Lee Shetterly

STEM Trailblazer Bios Book Series, by Lerner Publishing Group

The Boy Who Harnessed the Wind, by William Kamkwamba

Women in Science: 50 Fearless Pioneers Who Changed the World, by Rachel Ignotofsky

ABOUT THE AUTHOR

Tori Cameron is an elementary STEAM teacher who loves when students create in her classroom, the STEAM Lab. The STEAM Lab is full of busy students, background music, and maker messes. Tori loves every minute of teaching! She also hosts a podcast called *STEAM Up the Classroom*, which features conversations with educators about STEAM and education. She is a finalist for 2019 Massachusetts STEM Teacher of the Year. Tori lives in Massachusetts with her husband and two sons.

Connect with Tori on Twitter @steamuptheclrsm and Instagram @steamuptheclassroom, or on her website, steamuptheclassroom.com.

CPSIA information can be obtained
at www.ICGtesting.com
Printed in the USA
JSHW041908101121
20197JS00004B/4